The Pochin School Cookbook

The Pochin School Cookbook

Favourite recipes collected from families and celebrities in aid of Leukaemia Research

HAMLYN

The Pochin School and publishers would like to thank
everyone who contributed their favourite recipes to this book.
The recipes have been carefully checked but it has not been
possible to try them all out nor check all the sources and
the school and publishers hope that any similarities or
errors will be forgiven.

The artwork in the book has been drawn by
Oliver Taylor – who is responsible for the 'Chef O'Glace' pictures – and
by pupils of the Pochin School.

Published 1986 by Hamlyn Publishing,
a division of The Hamlyn Publishing Group Limited,
Bridge House, London Road, Twickenham, Middlesex, England

ISBN 0 600 32647 0

Set in Linotron Helvetica by
Wyvern Typesetting Limited, Bristol

Printed in Spain

Lito. A. Romero, S. A. – D. L. TF. 986 - 1986

CONTENTS

This book is dedicated to

Oliver Taylor

• a courageous boy •

who inspires all who know him

YORK HOUSE
ST. JAMES'S PALACE
LONDON S.W.1

I warmly congratulate the Pochin School on their enterprise in preparing this recipe book.

This valuable project is all the more appreciated in the knowledge that a pupil from the School is suffering from leukaemia and the proceeds from the sale of the book will go to help the Leukaemia Research Fund, of which I am the Patron, to combat this terrible disease.

I commend this recipe book to you in the hope that you will enjoy its culinary delights and thank you for your support for the work of the Leukaemia Research Fund.

Edward

His Royal Highness The Duke of Kent
Patron, The Leukaemia Research Fund

The Story behind the Book

Oliver Taylor contracted leukaemia during his first year at The Pochin School, in 1978 and has very bravely fought this disease from then to the present time.

Over the years his fellow pupils and the staff have seen him overcome the often embarrassing results of the unpleasant treatment he has had to undergo. They have seen how his courage has overcome long and frequent absences from school, to the extent that he has even received awards for high standards achieved in academic work.

His cheerful and determined personality is an inspiration to all who know him and so pupils and staff, together with parents of fellow pupils, decided to work to raise money to aid research into leukaemia and so one day combat this dreadful disease.

At first the book was to be a local affair to be sold at a school fund raising function, but as enthusiasm grew, and as Oliver's fight had to be strengthened, so the idea that greater benefit to the cause would be assured if it were published and sold on a national basis. A great undertaking for so small a village school. The task has at times proved a daunting one, but those concerned have been greatly encouraged by the kind people who have favoured us with their recipes, and by those persons and firms who have sponsored the enterprise. To each and everyone a very special thank you is extended for without such support this book would never have seen the light of day.

But the thanks of all concerned are also expressed to you who have so kindly purchased this book. You are helping a very worthy cause, giving hope to the many sufferers of leukaemia, and support to their families.

Mr P J Shelton
Headmaster
The Pochin School

Oliver's Story

I first discovered that I had leukaemia in September 1978, I am now 12 years old and can remember some very boring and stressful stays in hospital, some so stressful that I nearly blew my top! In fact once I actually did. I had had a relapse and was having radio therapy during dinner hour so I'd missed my dinner, that was all right because I don't like hospital food but my mum and dad bring me in food that I will eat, including my own cereals (Kelloggs CoCo Pops). I was up since 6.00 am the following morning watching breakfast TV and a nurse supposedly came in and supposedly saw me asleep, which I certainly wasn't! Anyway when a nurse did come in I blew my top and threw my breakfast all over the nurse and she wasn't very pleased! It was about now that I created Mr Pinstripe a very old yet crazy character who is always parking his car on double yellow lines. I was a third year junior at the same school at the time.

It was in this year of school I'd missed a whole term because I was in hospital but I came out fighting and won the academic cup for my year, and I also passed my cycle proficiency test with flying colours. The next year was my fourth and final year at the school but it proved vital in my further education as I came third overall in the exams after having lots of time off school and I was asked to come up with a character for a recipe book. I didn't know then that it was going to be for Leukaemia Research and Pinstripe changed into Chef O Glacé.

Any time my present school is on strike and I'm not at hospital, I'm at the Pochin School helping out. The first picture I came up with was simply Pinstripe hiding behind a rather large cup cake.

All I am saying here is keep fighting, keep calm, don't be afraid and don't throw your food at the doctors or nurses because they might resign like the one who had my breakfast thrown all over her did! The school are very good and every year they do a sponsored silence. One year they did it for Leukaemia Research and this year they did it for the book which will raise money for Leukaemia also.

· SOUPS ·

Plum and Cherry Soup

• Serves 6–8 •

450 g/1 lb plums, halved and stoned

275 g/10 oz cherries, halved and stoned

225 g/8 oz pears, halved and cored

50 g/2 oz sugar

½ teaspoon salt

1 teaspoon ground cinnamon

juice and finely grated rind of 1 lemon

1.15 litres/2 pints water

1 teaspoon cornflour

Place the fruit in a large saucepan and add the sugar, salt, cinnamon, lemon juice and rind. Pour in the water, bring to the boil over a high heat, stirring well. Reduce the heat, cover and cook for 10 minutes or until the fruit is tender. Remove from the heat, blend and strain. Return to the pan, mix the cornflour to a paste with a little of the liquid and add a little at a time to the soup. Boil again for 5 to 8 minutes. Serve very cold.

• **Contributed by Olive Wells** •
TTTE RAF Cottesmore

Contributed by

Elizabeth Peacock-Pochin

Pea Soup

• Serves 4–5 •

25 g/1 oz butter

1 small onion, finely chopped

225 g/8 oz fresh or frozen peas

600 ml/1 pint good chicken stock

8 mint leaves

1 teaspoon caster sugar

salt and freshly ground black pepper

1 tablespoon single cream to serve (optional)

Melt the butter in a large saucepan and add the onion. Cook over a gentle heat until the onion has softened, but do not allow to brown. Add the peas, stock and mint leaves and simmer gently for 10 minutes. Add the sugar and season to taste with salt and pepper. Blend the soup in a food processor or liquidiser. Reheat the soup or leave to chill, as preferred. Stir in the cream just before serving, if using.

Contributed by

Blue Peter, BBC

French Onion Soup

• Serves 4 •

8 medium onions
50 g/2 oz butter
1 tablespoon oil
2 tablespoons flour
900 ml/1½ pints water
salt and pepper
Garnish
8 slices bread
75 g/3 oz butter
100 g/ 4 oz cheese, grated

Peel and thinly slice the onions. (A good tip when you peel them is to leave the ends on the onion, so the rings don't fall apart when you slice it up.)

Melt the butter and oil in a saucepan and add the onions. Cook the onions for 20 minutes over a medium heat until they are a golden brown and all the liquid has evaporated. (This is called reducing and when completed the onions should take up a quarter of the space they did at the start.) Leave the pan uncovered and stir from time to time to stop the onions sticking to the bottom. Add the flour and stir into the onions. Leave the mixture over a low heat for 10 minutes to thicken, stirring occasionally.

Add the water and stir the mixture well. Leave to cook over a medium heat for 40 minutes, stirring occasionally. When cooked season with salt and pepper to taste.

Just before the soup has finished cooking, gently fry the slices of bread in the butter. Keep turning so that the butter soaks through. Pour the soup into a heatproof dish. Put the fried bread slices on top and sprinkle with the grated cheese. Put under a hot grill for about 30 seconds or until the cheese has melted.

The Rt Hon
NIGEL LAWSON
MP

JOHN CRAVEN

Parsnip Soup

• Serves 4 •

1 very large parsnip

75 g / 3 oz butter

100 g / 4 oz finely chopped onion

1 clove garlic, crushed

1 tablespoon flour

1 tablespoon good quality curry powder

1.15 litres / 2 pints hot beef stock

150 ml / ¼ pint single cream

chives to garnish, if available

croûtons to serve

Peel and slice the parsnip and cook it very gently with the butter, onion and garlic in a heavy saucepan, keeping the lid on. The vegetables shouldn't brown just soften. Add the flour and curry powder to take up the fat, stirring with a wooden spoon, and gradually incorporate the hot stock. Simmer until the parsnip is cooked. Allow to cool slightly and then blend until smooth in a food processor or liquidiser. Return to the saucepan, correct the seasoning and then stir in the cream. Decant the soup and sprinkle the chives (if available) over the top. Serve with croûtons.

• **Obtained by Samantha Carnall** •

Favourite Soup

• Serves 4–6 •

2.25 litres / 4 pints cold water

3 chicken stock cubes

2 carrots, coarsely grated

2 leeks, cleaned, split lengthways and finely sliced

2 onions, finely chopped

a little chopped cabbage or celery (optional)

2 tablespoons concentrated tomato purée or 4 large tomatoes, peeled, deseeded and chopped

salt and ground black pepper

a few strands of spaghetti or rice

Put the first six ingredients in a large pan, bring to the boil, simmer for one hour, adding more water if necessary. After 30 minutes add either the tomato purée or the chopped tomatoes. Season to taste with salt and pepper.

Before reheating for 5 to 10 minutes, add a few strands of spaghetti, crushed in your hand, or rice.

• **Obtained by David Harris** •

PAUL McCARTNEY

Green Pea Soup

• **Serves 8–10** •

675 g/1½ lb green split peas

450 g/1 lb orange lentils

3 large onions, quartered

1 head of celery, including leaves

4 peeled tomatoes

4 leeks

(plus any other suitable left-over vegetables)

225 g/8 oz butter

Place the split peas, lentils, onions, celery, tomatoes, leeks and any other vegetables you may have in a large saucepan. Cover with water then add another 900 ml/ 1½ pints. Simmer until soft (about 3 hours). You can blend this soup in a food processor or liquidiser if you want a very smooth soup. When ready add butter and salt and pepper to taste. Stir well and eat immediately.

ESTHER RANTZEN

Consommé Pettifer

• **Serves 6** •

2 (411-g/14-oz) cans consommé

about 150 ml/¼ pint double cream

mock caviar (lumpfish roe) to garnish

lemon slices to serve

Pour the consommé into six bowls or glasses and chill until set. Whip the double cream. Put one dollop on each bowl or glass of jellied consommé. Sprinkle the mock caviar on the cream. Hang a slice of lemon on the rim of each bowl.

• **Obtained by the School** •

❛ This may not be cheap, but it tastes delicious, and it is not very time consuming. With very best wishes for every success with your recipes. ❜

• *FISH* •

Janice Long

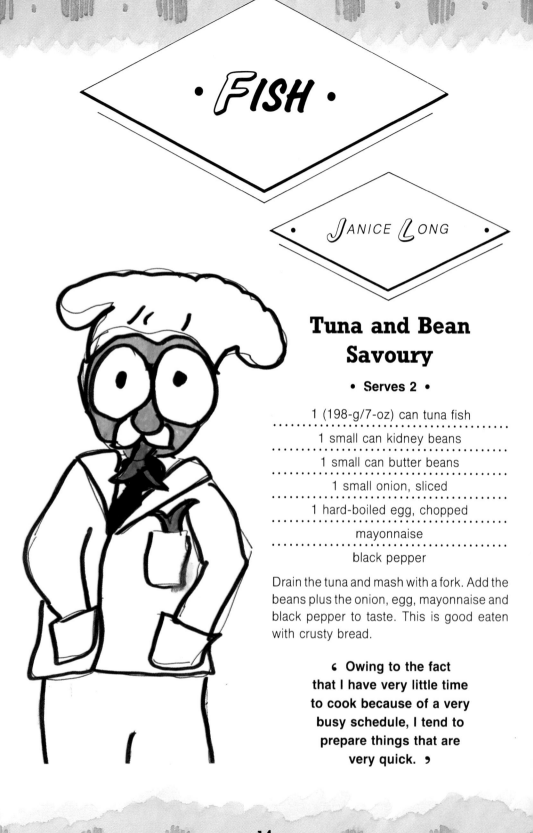

Tuna and Bean Savoury

• Serves 2 •

1 (198-g/7-oz) can tuna fish

1 small can kidney beans

1 small can butter beans

1 small onion, sliced

1 hard-boiled egg, chopped

mayonnaise

black pepper

Drain the tuna and mash with a fork. Add the beans plus the onion, egg, mayonnaise and black pepper to taste. This is good eaten with crusty bread.

❝ Owing to the fact that I have very little time to cook because of a very busy schedule, I tend to prepare things that are very quick. ❞

JAN LEEMING

Mackerel Mousse

· **Serves 6–8 as a starter** ·

1 (425-g/15-oz) can mackerel
(for a more splendid occasion use a tin of salmon)

2 sticks celery, finely chopped

1 tablespoon capers

150 ml/¼ pint double cream, whipped

salt and pepper to taste

1 teaspoon mustard powder

1 teaspoon powdered gelatine

1 tablespoon wine vinegar

3 tablespoons water

1 tablespoon sugar

a fish ring or mould

Mix together the first five ingredients in a bowl. Either put the remainder in a non-stick saucepan and gently heat until gelatine has dissolved or put the ingredients in a small heatproof bowl, place in boiling water, lower the heat and simmer until gelatine dissolves. Pour liquid into bowl with other ingredients and mix well.

Wet mould under cold water. Spoon in ingredients and place in fridge to set. Can be decorated by putting a layer of tomato or cucumber on bottom of mould. This is an ideal dish to freeze.

· **Obtained by Caroline Lilley** ·

❛ **This is a recipe that I enjoy making and eating myself. Best wishes with the fund raising.** ❜

Duchess of Wellington

Stratfield Saye Trout

• Serves 2 •

1 medium trout, cleaned

2 tablespoons chopped mint

2 tablespoons chopped parsley

1 clove garlic, crushed

grated rind and juice of 1 lemon

salt and pepper

Stuff the trout with the mint, parsley, garlic, lemon rind and juice, salt and pepper mixed together. Allow to stand in a cool place for about 30 minutes.

Fry in melted butter for 5 minutes each side. When ready, garnish with chopped parsley and slices of lemon.

Pick young nettle shoots, cook in boiling salted water until tender and use as an accompaniment to the trout. If liked, make a rich cheese sauce and pour over.

• **Obtained by Samantha Lilley** •

❛ We are lucky enough to be able to catch the trout in our little river, and of course living in the country there is an abundant supply of young nettle shoots. ❜

Fisherman's Pie

• Serves 4–6 •

1 (425-g/15-oz) can pilchards

4 hard-boiled eggs, chopped

1 (425-g/15-oz) can chopped tomatoes

1 kg/2 lb potatoes, boiled and mashed

50 g/2 oz butter, melted

1 beaten egg

salt and pepper

White Sauce

25 g/1 oz butter

25 g/1 oz flour

600 ml/1 pint milk

Make the white sauce first by melting the butter in a saucepan then adding the flour. Cook for a few minutes then gradually add the milk, stirring continuously. Flake the pilchards and mix with the eggs and white sauce. Place in an ovenproof dish with the tomatoes. Beat the potatoes, butter and egg together and season well. Pipe or pile on top of the fish mixture and bake in a moderately hot oven (190 C, 375 F, gas 5) for 30 minutes, until golden.

• **Contributed by Mrs Joyce Mount** •

$\mathcal{B}$OBBY $\mathcal{B}$ALL

Fish in Cheese Sauce

• **Serves 4** •

450 g/1 lb white fish fillets

salt and pepper

about 25 g/1 oz butter

2 tablespoons lemon juice

2 tablespoons white wine

900 g/2 lb potatoes

2 tomatoes

1 packet cheese sauce mix

Skin the fish or ask your fishmonger to do it for you. Put into a casserole dish and season with salt and pepper. Cover with a few knobs of butter. Pour over the lemon juice and white wine. Put aluminium foil over the dish, or cover with the lid, and cook in a moderately hot oven (200 C, 400 F, gas 6) for 25 minutes. While the fish is cooking, peel the potatoes and boil for 20 minutes. Peel the tomatoes and slice thinly. When the fish is cooked drain off the juices and add to the liquid used to make the cheese sauce. Pour the sauce over the fish. Mash the potatoes and pipe around the edge of the casserole dish. Put the sliced tomatoes in the middle and bake in a hot oven (220 C, 425 F, gas 7) for a few minutes until the potatoes are golden brown.

Note

To make a cheese sauce, melt 15 g/½ oz butter then stir in 15 g/½ oz flour and cook over a low heat for a couple of minutes. Gradually add 300 ml/½ pint milk and the cooking juices from the fish. Finally, mix in 75 g/3 oz grated Cheddar cheese and season to taste.

BOY GEORGE

'Boil in a Bag'

One packet of 'Cod in Parsley Sauce'

Place in boiling water. Bring to boil.
Simmer for 20 minutes. Serve

**❝ This may add some
light humour to your book,
it sounds brilliant. Good
luck. ❞**

• Obtained by Lucy Pick •
ex Headgirl

Contributed by

Lord and Lady Gretton

Prawn Pappadam Specials

• Serves 4 •

4 tablespoons mayonnaise

2 teaspoons curry powder

pinch of ground ginger

100 g/4 oz peeled cooked prawns, defrosted if frozen

2 hard-boiled eggs

fried pappadams

Mix together the mayonnaise, curry powder and ginger then add the prawns. Chop the hard-boiled eggs and stir into the mixture. Turn the mixture into a serving bowl.

To serve – let each person help themselves and spread on to the freshly fried pappadams. This can be used as a starter or as a light lunch or supper dish.

**❝ We look forward to
reading and using the
book and wish every
success for such a
worthwhile cause. ❞**

• ⒼORDON Ⓜ ILNE •

Hasty Prawn Curry

• Serves 4 •

1 large onion

25 g/1 oz butter

15 g/½ oz flour

2 teaspoons curry powder

1 tablespoon mango chutney

450 ml/¾ pint water

1 dessert apple, peeled, cored and chopped

100 g/4 oz peeled cooked prawns, defrosted if frozen

2 (439-g/15½-oz) cans curried beans with sultanas

100–150 g/4–6 oz Patna rice

1 teaspoon turmeric

a few whole prawns to garnish (optional)

Chop the onion and fry in the butter until lightly browned. Blend the flour, curry powder and chutney together with a little of the water, add to the onion and cook for 3 minutes, stirring all the time. Add the rest of the water and the chopped apple and bring to the boil. Leave to simmer gently for 10 to 15 minutes, adding the prawns and beans after 10 minutes.

Meanwhile, cook the rice with the turmeric in boiling salted water for 15 minutes. Drain the rice and arrange on a serving dish with the curry in the middle, garnish with a few unshelled prawns, if liked.

(As a variation, use hard-boiled eggs instead of prawns or a mixture of prawns, eggs and shrimps. Instead of shellfish use white fish, skin and cut this into neat pieces then put into the curry sauce and cook for about 8 minutes until tender, but unbroken. The curry sauce can be stored and the prawns added when re-heating.)

ARCHBISHOP OF CANTERBURY

Helen's Seafood Pancakes

• Serves 4 •

225 g/8 oz cod

225 g/8 oz smoked haddock

3 tablespoons white wine

1 lemon, sliced

½ onion, sliced

225 g/8 oz peeled cooked prawns, defrosted if frozen

1 tablespoon brandy

25 g/1 oz butter

25 g/1 oz flour

150 ml/¼ pint double cream

a little grated cheese

salt and pepper

Pancake Batter

100 g/4 oz flour

½ teaspoon salt

300 ml/½ pint milk

1 large egg

butter for frying

Place the flour, salt, milk and egg in a food processor or liquidiser and blend until smooth. Stand for 30 minutes then make the pancakes by frying a little batter at a time in a heavy-based frying pan. Make 16 pancakes and keep them warm.

Poach the fish gently for about 10 minutes in the wine, lemon and onion, adding sufficient water to cover the fish. Reserve the stock and strain. Flake the fish into a bowl and add the prawns. Flambé the brandy and pour over the fish.

Make a binding sauce with the butter, flour and reserved stock. Cool, then add cream and seasoning to taste. Use half the sauce to bind the fish together. Fill the pancakes and place on a greased ovenproof dish. Coat with the remaining sauce. Sprinkle with grated cheese and heat in a hot oven (220 C, 425 F, gas 7) for 10 minutes. Serve immediately.

· DALEY THOMPSON ·

Seafood Salad

• Serves 6–8 •

225 g/8 oz lightly cooked white fish
(e.g. cod, haddock, monkfish, mullet)

1 lobster or 1 crab

600 ml/1 pint mussels

4–6 oysters

4–6 scallops

225 g/8 oz peeled cooked prawns or
Dublin Bay prawns (scampi)

lemon wedges to serve

Salad

1 crisp lettuce

1 endive

watercress

cucumber

spring onions

Dressing

3 tablespoons olive or sunflower oil

1 tablespoon lemon juice

½ teaspoon prepared mustard

salt and pepper

Prepare the fish by removing any bones and skin and chopping the flesh into large chunks. Extract the meat from the lobster or crab. Cook the mussels, having removed their 'beards', by steaming open in a little fish stock or water.

The oysters do not need cooking – simply prise open the shells. Open the scallops and extract the white flesh and coral and cook gently in a little butter for a few minutes. Do not overcook.

Make a green salad with all the ingredients listed. Make up the dressing by putting all the ingredients in a screw-top jar and shaking well to combine. Add the dressing to the salad and toss well to coat the salad well. Arrange the salad on a large platter and pile the mixed seafood on top. Serve with lemon wedges.

❛ Depending on which country I am in the ingredients inevitably vary. Use a selection of fish and shellfish in this recipe depending upon taste and availability. ❜

• POULTRY •

Chicken Provençale

• Serves 4 •

4 boneless chicken breasts

100 g/4 oz butter, chilled

1 beaten egg

breadcrumbs to coat

50 g/2 oz capers

1 (397-g/14-oz) can chopped tomatoes

1 teaspoon herbes de provence

4 medium carrots, sliced

225 g/8 oz button mushrooms

salt and pepper

a knob of butter

Flatten out the chicken breasts and put 25 g/1 oz of the chilled butter in the centre of each. Parcel up and secure each with a wooden cocktail stick. Coat well in egg and breadcrumbs. Place all the ingredients in a roasting tin with a knob of butter. Season with salt and pepper. Cover the roasting tin with aluminium foil and bake in a moderately hot oven (190 C, 375 F, gas 5) for about 40 to 50 minutes, or until the chicken is tender.

Chicken Tikka

• Serves 4 •

450 g/1 lb boneless chicken breast

300 ml/½ pint natural yogurt

1 clove garlic, crushed

1 (2.5-cm/1-in) cube root ginger, grated

2 teaspoons garam masala

2 teaspoons paprika

2 green chillies, deseeded and finely chopped (optional)

1 teaspoon ground coriander

1 teaspoon salt

Cut the chicken into chunks and place in a bowl. Mix the yogurt with the remaining ingredients, pour over the chicken and mix well until all the chicken pieces are coated with the sauce. Cover and marinate for 2 to 24 hours in a refrigerator.

Grill for 8 to 12 minutes on skewers. A slice of onion can be placed on the skewer between each chicken piece. Serve with lemon wedges, rice and green salad.

• **Contributed by Julia Joint** •
TTTE RAF Cottesmore

Contributed by

Dr JK Wood, FRCPE MRCPUK FRCPath

Consultant Haematologist,
Leicester Royal Infirmary, Leicester

❝ **Popular with
supper parties and may be
prepared in advance.** ❞

Chicken with Rice and Nuts

• **Serves 4** •

12 chicken drumsticks
melted butter to brush
1 lemon
1 orange
450 ml/¾ pint chicken stock
salt and pepper
225 g/8 oz long-grain rice
50 g/2 oz butter
25 g/1 oz peanuts, pistachio or cashew nuts
50 g/2 oz stoned raisins

Brush the drumsticks with melted butter and roast in a moderately hot oven (200 C, 400 F, gas 6) for 45 minutes. Meanwhile, remove the peel from the lemon and orange and finely shred. Squeeze the lemon and add the juice to the stock seasoned with a little salt and pepper to taste. Simmer the rice until tender in this mixture. Add the butter, nuts, raisins and shredded peel to the rice and keep hot. Pile the rice on a serving dish and place drumsticks around in a crown formation. Re-heat if necessary. Serve with a tossed green salad.

· NANCY REAGAN ·

Baja California Chicken

• Serves 8 •

8 boneless chicken breasts

salt and pepper to taste

2 cloves garlic, crushed

4 tablespoons olive oil

4 tablespoons tarragon vinegar

150 ml / ¼ pint dry sherry

Sprinkle the chicken with salt and pepper. Mix the crushed garlic with the oil and vinegar and place in a skillet or frying pan. Sauté the chicken pieces until golden brown, turning frequently. Remove; place in a baking dish. Pour the sherry over the chicken and place in a moderate oven (180 C, 350 F, gas 4) for 10 minutes.

Chicken on Mushrooms

• Serves 4 •

100 g / 4 oz mushrooms, sliced

450 ml / ¾ pint chicken stock

4 chicken breasts

4 rashers rindless streaky bacon

25 g / 1 oz butter

150 ml / ¼ pint white wine

Sauce

25 g / 1 oz butter

25 g / 1 oz flour

about 600 ml / 1 pint chicken stock from the casserole

Sprinkle the bottom of an ovenproof dish with the mushrooms. Pour on the stock. Parcel the chicken breasts with bacon and place on the mushrooms. Add a knob of butter to each parcel. Pour the wine over the top. Cook for 1 hour in a moderately hot oven (190 C, 375 F, gas 5).

To make the sauce melt the butter in a pan and add the flour. Strain the liquid from chicken and add to the roux and pour over the chicken parcels. Serve immediately.

• **Contributed by Mrs Audrey Mount** •

Forrester's Casserole

• Serves 4 •

4 chicken joints

50 g/2 oz butter

1 large onion

225 g/8 oz button mushrooms

2 tablespoons plain flour

300 ml/½ pint apple juice

150 ml/¼ pint chicken stock

salt and black pepper

bouquet garni

2–3 tablespoons cream

Fry the chicken joints in half the butter until golden brown all over. Transfer to a casserole dish. Peel and chop the onion and fry in the remaining butter until just transparent. Add the mushrooms, cook until tender. Sprinkle in the flour, gradually blend in the apple juice and stock. Stir over a gentle heat until the sauce thickens. Season well and pour over the chicken. Add the bouquet garni. Cover and cook in a moderately hot oven (180 C, 350 F, gas 4) for 1 to 1½ hours. Stir in the cream just before serving.

• Contributed by Mrs Bevan •

SUE LAWLEY

Spicy Chicken

• Serves 4 •

1 chicken

450 ml/¾ pint double cream

4 tablespoons mushroom ketchup

8 tablespoons Worcestershire sauce

2–3 teaspoons prepared English mustard

Roast the chicken – let it go cold, then skin and joint it. Lay the joints in a shallow ovenproof dish. Whizz up the double cream with the mushroom ketchup, Worcestershire sauce, and a couple of teaspoons of English mustard. Smear the mixture all over the joints and bake it all in a hot oven (220 C, 425 F, gas 7) for 40 minutes, until bubbly and brown on top.

• Obtained by Henry Mount •

Chicken or Turkey à La King

• **Serves 3–4** •

A delicious
method of using left-overs.

1 green pepper

50 g/2 oz butter

100 g/4 oz mushrooms, sliced

1 tablespoon flour

300 ml/½ pint chicken stock

150 ml/¼ pint milk

1 teaspoon salt

freshly ground pepper

350 g/12 oz cooked chicken or turkey,
cut into chunks

150 ml/¼ pint single cream

2 egg yolks

Deseed the green pepper, removing the pith, and chop. Melt the butter in a frying pan and sauté the chopped pepper for 5 minutes then add the sliced mushrooms. Remove the pan from the heat and stir in the flour. Gradually add the stock and milk and, stirring continuously, heat to boil and thicken. Season with salt and pepper, add the pieces of chicken and heat through. Blend together the cream and egg yolks and stir into the sauce – do not boil from this point on. Serve with rice or in vol-au-vent cases.

• **Contributed by Maggie Dougherty** •
TTTE RAF Cottesmore

E NGLEBERT
H UMPERDINCK

Scalloped Chicken à La Humperdinck

• Serves 4 •

1½ tablespoons butter or margarine

50 g/2 oz slivered almonds

1 packet mushroom soup mix

2 tablespoons flour

450 ml/¾ pint milk

450 g/1 lb cooked potatoes, sliced

450 g/1 lb cooked chicken, chopped

350 g/12 oz cooked carrots, sliced

In a medium saucepan, melt the butter or margarine and sauté the slivered almonds until golden. Stir in the packet mushroom soup mix blended with the flour and milk. Bring to the boil, then simmer, stirring constantly, until the sauce is slightly thickened, about 5 minutes. In a greased 1.15-litres/2-pints casserole, layer half the sliced cooked potatoes, half the cut-up chicken and half the cooked carrots, plus half the sauce.

Repeat with the remaining potatoes, chicken and carrots and top with the remaining sauce. Bake in a moderate oven (180 C, 350 F, gas 4) for 30 minutes or until heated through.

Herby Chickenburgers

• Serves 2–4 •

225 g/8 oz cooked chicken, minced

50 g/2 oz grated onion

1 teaspoon dried mixed herbs

275 g/10 oz cottage cheese, sieved

salt and pepper

Mix all ingredients thoroughly, shape into four flat cakes and chill for 1 hour. Place under a hot grill and cook each side for 5 minutes, or until golden and heated through.

• **Contributed by Jan Creedy** •

Chicken Satay

• Serves 6 •

Satay is an Indonesian speciality popular in South China and Malaya, also popular among the diners at the Station.

Satay can be made with beef, pork, veal or poultry. The meat should be cut into bite-size pieces, skewered and grilled.

1½ teaspoons salt

pepper to taste

1.5 kg / 3 lb boneless chicken, skinned and cut into bite-size pieces

3–4 tablespoons peanut butter

1 teaspoon chilli powder

1 teaspoon grated lemon rind

1½ teaspoons brown sugar

300 ml / ½ pint hot water

juice of ½ lime or lemon

Coconut Cream

100 g / 4 oz desiccated coconut

6 tablespoons water or milk

First make the coconut cream by combining the coconut and water and pressing through a sieve. Add the salt, pepper and the bite-sized chicken and marinate for at least 1 hour.

Place 3 or 4 pieces of chicken on to skewers. Baste the skewered chicken with the marinade then grill the chicken, basting with the marinade as you cook.

Put the peanut butter, chilli powder, lemon rind, brown sugar and water into a saucepan and bring to the boil. Reduce the heat and simmer for 15 minutes. Remove from the heat and stir in the lime or lemon juice.

Place the cooked and skewered chicken on to a dish and spoon a little of the sauce over each skewer. Serve the remainder of the sauce separately. Allow 2 to 3 skewers per person. Fried rice may be served if desired.

• **Contributed by the Officers' Mess** •
RAF North Luffenham

Curried Chicken

• Serves 4 •

1 (1.25-kg/2½-lb) chicken

salt

about 50 g/2 oz fat

225 g/8 oz chopped onion

1 clove garlic, crushed

15 g/½ oz flour

15 g/½ oz curry powder

1 tablespoon concentrated tomato purée

600 ml/1 pint chicken stock

15 g/½ oz sultanas

25 g/1 oz chopped chutney

50 g/2 oz chopped apple

2–3 tablespoons desiccated coconut

1 small carton natural yogurt (optional)

Cut the chicken into portions and season with salt. Heat the fat (either butter or oil) in a sauté or frying pan then add the chicken and lightly brown on both sides. Add the chopped onion and garlic. Cover with a lid and cook gently for 3 to 4 minutes. Mix in the flour and curry powder then mix in the tomato purée. Add the stock and bring to the boil. Skim off any excess fat using a spoon or kitchen paper. Add the remainder of the ingredients. Simmer until cooked. The sauce can be finished with a carton of natural yogurt, if wished. Serve with plain boiled rice, offering Bombay duck, diced onion/tomato, poppadums etc.

• **Contributed by the Officers' Mess** •
RAF North Luffenham

Pheasant with Green Apples

• Serves 2–3 •

100 g/4 oz rindless bacon, diced

½ Spanish onion, finely chopped

1 clove garlic, finely chopped

2 tablespoons butter

2 tablespoons corn oil

1 pheasant

4 cooking apples, peeled and cored

4 tablespoons Cointreau

salt and freshly ground black pepper

300 ml/½ pint cream

Sauté the bacon, onion and garlic in the butter and oil. Remove from the pan and brown the pheasant in the fat. Slice the apples thickly and sauté in the remaining fat. Pour over the Cointreau. Skim the fat from pan juices. Place all these ingredients in a flameproof casserole and simmer on the hob, covered, for 10 minutes. Add salt and pepper to taste and cook in a moderate oven (180 C, 350 F, gas 4) for 50 to 60 minutes.

To serve, remove pheasant, bacon and onion from the casserole and keep hot. Purée the sauce and apples, then add the cream. Reheat gently and pour over the pheasant.

• **Contributed by Betty Green** •
TTTE RAF Cottesmore

· MEAT ·

· RONNIE BARKER ·

Barbecued Spareribs

• Serves 4 •

1 kg/2 lb pork spareribs

5 tablespoons concentrated tomato purée

2 tablespoons clear honey

2 tablespoons soy sauce

3 tablespoons red wine vinegar

300 ml/½ pint beef stock

pinch of salt

Spread the ribs in a single layer in a large ovenproof dish. Mix all the remaining ingredients together. Pour the mixture over the ribs and turn so that all sides are coated. Leave in a cool place for 3 hours, turning the ribs occasionally. Roast the ribs in a moderately hot oven (200 C, 400 F, gas 6) in the marinade for 1 hour, turning and basting from time to time. Reduce the heat to moderate (180 C, 350 F, gas 4) and roast the ribs, covered, for a further hour, basting from time to time.

John Inman

'Boeuf en Croute' or Beef Wellington

• Serves 4–6 •

15 g/½ oz butter

1 small onion, finely chopped

100 g/4 oz mushrooms, finely chopped

salt and pepper to taste

1 teaspoon concentrated tomato purée

2 tablespoons red wine or 1 tablespoon brandy

1 kg/2 lb piece beef fillet

1 tablespoon corn oil

450 g/1 lb frozen puff pastry, defrosted

1 beaten egg to glaze

To make the filling – melt the butter, fry the chopped onion and mushrooms, add salt and pepper to taste, stir in the tomato purée and red wine or brandy, and continue cooking until the alcohol has evaporated. Allow to cool.

Trim the fillet, brush with corn oil and place on a baking sheet in a hot oven (200 C, 400 F, gas 6) for 10 minutes, to seal the surfaces of the meat. Cool.

Roll out the pastry into an oblong shape large enough to wrap the steak in. Trim a little off the end for decoration. Place the fillet in the centre of the pastry and cover with the filling. Fold the pastry to centre, dampen the edges and seal. Turn over, seal the ends and trim. Use the reserved pastry trimmings for decoration, dampen slightly to attach. Brush with a little beaten egg to glaze and bake in a hot oven (220 C, 425 F, gas 7) for about 30 minutes. Pastry should be golden brown and the fillet *rare.* Garnish with parsley and serve with a green salad or vegetables, as desired.

• **Obtained by Mr P J Shelton** •

❛ **I am delighted to help with your fund raising and the recipe is enclosed herewith. I wish you well with your endeavours.** ❜

BARRY **S**HEENE

Steak au Poivre

• Serves 4 •

48 black peppercorns

about 150 ml / ¼ pint brandy

4 (225-g / 8-oz) rump steaks

beef suet or oil

salt

Crush the peppercorns coarsely. Put the crushed peppercorns into a screw-top jar, sprinkle with 1 tablespoon brandy. Screw lid on and shake vigorously. Leave to marinate for 3 hours.

Take the steaks out of the fridge and leave to come to room temperature. Press generous amounts of the marinated peppercorns into both sides of the steaks.

Heat a frying pan until a tiny bit of water evaporates on contact. Rub a piece of beef suet or the oil on a wad of kitchen paper all over the base and sides of pan. The grease should start to smoke. Slap the steaks into the pan. Turn quickly to seal on both sides. Reduce the heat and cook to taste. Transfer to a hot serving plate and sprinkle with a little salt. Put the remaining brandy in the pan, stir briefly, and scrape the sides and base of the pan. Pour the hot brandy over the steaks and serve immediately.

Beef Stew with Herb and Horseradish Dumplings

• **Serves 6–8** •

1.25 kg / 2½ lb stewing beef

12 button onions

450 g / 1 lb carrots

50 g / 2 oz dripping or cooking fat

3 bay leaves

50 g / 2 oz plain flour

300 ml / ½ pint red wine

2 cloves garlic, crushed

sprig each of marjoram and parsley

salt and pepper

600–900 ml / 1–1 ½ pints water

Dumplings

100 g / 4 oz plain flour

1½ teaspoons baking powder

100 g / 4 oz shredded suet

1 tablespoon dried mixed herbs

1 tablespoon grated horseradish (optional)

1 large egg, beaten

a little milk

Trim any fat from the beef and cut into cubes. Peel the onions and carrots and slice the latter into rings. Melt the dripping or cooking fat in a pan, add the bay leaves and onions and fry for 2 minutes. Place the onions in an ovenproof casserole and discard the bay leaves. Toss the beef in the hot fat and fry until brown all over. Sprinkle in the flour and stir well until meat is evenly coated. Pour in the red wine. Add the sliced carrots, garlic, marjoram and parsley. Stir in seasoning to taste and the water. Bring to the boil, then turn into the casserole with the onions. Cover and cook in a moderate oven (160 C, 325 F, gas 3) for 2 to 2½ hours or until the meat is tender.

Meanwhile, prepare the dumplings, sift the flour and baking powder into a bowl. Add the shredded suet, salt, pepper, mixed herbs and grated horseradish, if using. Mix to a soft dough with beaten egg and milk. Divide the mixture into small pieces and roll into balls with floured hands.

About 30 minutes before the stew is to be served, turn up the oven temperature to hot (220 C, 425 F, gas 7) and place the dumplings on top of the meat. Replace the lid but take it off 5 minutes before serving to brown the dumplings.

• **Contributed by Mr P J Shelton** •

Steak and Kidney Pudding

• Serves 6 •

675 g/1½ lb rump steak or good quality beef steak

225 g/8 oz lambs' kidneys

40 g/1½ oz seasoned flour

450 ml/¾ pint beef or veal stock

1 onion, chopped

parsley (optional)

225 g/8 oz button mushrooms

Suet Crust Pastry

275 g/10 oz self-raising flour

1 teaspoon baking powder

¼ teaspoon salt

freshly ground white pepper

150 g/5 oz chopped suet

cold water to mix

First make the pastry. Sift together the flour, baking powder and seasoning then add the chopped suet. Mix well and add sufficient water to form a firm dough.

Trim the steak of all fat and sinew and cut into 2.5-cm/1-in cubes. Flatten each piece with a meat hammer. Skin and core the kidney and dice it. Roll pieces of steak in the seasoned flour, put a piece of kidney on each and roll each piece up. Line a large, well-greased pudding basin with the suet pastry, leaving a circle to form the lid. Place in the rolls of meat and cover with the beef or veal stock. Sprinkle on the onions, parsley and mushrooms then place in remaining meat rolls. Just cover with half the remaining stock, reserving the rest to add to the pudding water. Put on lid, damping top edge of the crust with cold water to make it stick. Cover the basin with buttered foil or greaseproof paper and place a small plate over the top. Place the basin in a saucepan. Half fill with water, bring to the boil and steam the pudding for 3 hours. Do not let pudding off the boil and top up with water from time to time to keep up the level.

When the pudding has cooked, bring the reserved stock up to the boil. Serve the pudding in the basin with a napkin pinned around it. Before serving make a small incision and pour in a little stock. Pour the rest of the stock into a jug and add to the pudding after each serving.

• Obtained by David Harris •

Beef and Bean Pancakes

• **Serves 4** •

You can also try chicken in white sauce instead of the beef and bean filling.

1 (198-g/7-oz) can corned beef

15 g/½ oz butter

1 (220-g/7¾-oz) can baked beans

1 (298-g/10½-oz) can condensed tomato soup

milk

25 g/1 oz Cheddar cheese, grated

Pancake Batter

100 g/4 oz plain flour

pinch of salt

1 egg

300 ml/½ pint milk

a little butter for frying

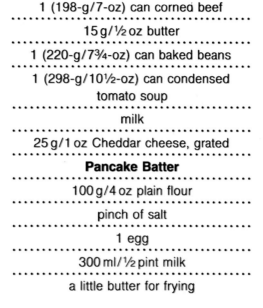

Make up 8 pancakes from the batter mixture, frying in a little butter. Gently fry the corned beef in the butter for 2 minutes. Stir in the baked beans and cook for a further minute. Stuff the pancakes with the mixture. Place in an ovenproof dish.

Reconstitute the soup with milk, heat and pour over the pancakes. Sprinkle with the grated cheese. Bake in a moderately hot oven (190 C, 375 F, gas 5) for 15 to 20 minutes. Serve hot with vegetables in season or a salad.

• **Contributed by Mrs Joyce Mount** •

Oxo Pie

• Serves 4 •

Delicious served either hot or cold

450 g/1 lb beef sausages

1 tablespoon oil

1 onion, chopped

100 g/4 oz mushrooms, sliced

2–3 tomatoes, sliced

4 eggs

1 Oxo cube, crumbled

beaten egg to glaze

Pastry

275 g/10 oz self-raising flour

pinch of salt

175 g/6 oz fat (lard and margarine)

1 Oxo cube (crumbled)

water to mix

First make the pastry. Sieve the flour and salt into a basin. Rub in the fat until it resembles fine breadcrumbs then add the crumbled cube. Stir in enough water to make a stiff dough. Roll out two-thirds of the pastry and use to line an 18 × 28-cm/7 × 11-in baking tin.

Cut the sausages into half lengthways and arrange on the base of the tin. Heat the oil and fry the onion and mushrooms until just tender, drain and spread over the sausages. Arrange the tomato slices over the onion mixture. Beat together the eggs and cube and pour over the sausages. Cover with the remaining pastry. Press down the edges well and decorate with pastry leaves. Brush with beaten egg. Bake in a moderately hot oven (200 C, 400 F, gas 6) for 10 minutes. Reduce the temperature to moderate (180 C, 350 F, gas 4) and cook for a further 30 minutes.

• **Contributed by Mrs L Hogg** •

Pressure-cooker Bolognese

• Serves 4 •

1 onion

450 g / 1 lb minced beef

1–2 tablespoons oil

1 (397-g / 14-oz) can chopped tomatoes or equivalent in fresh tomatoes

1 beef stock cube, crumbled

paprika

dash of vinegar (optional)

1 tablespoon cornflour

Chop the onion and fry gently with the meat in a little cooking oil in the open pressure cooker until the meat has lost its 'raw' look. Add the tomatoes and sufficient water to cover the ingredients. Add the beef cube and paprika to taste. (If a sharper flavour is required add a dash of vinegar.) Cover the pan and cook on high pressure for 10 minutes. Mix the cornflour with a little water and thicken the bolognese after it is cooked. Serve piping hot with spaghetti.

• **Contributed by Mrs F Wesson** •

· $\mathcal{T}$ONY $\mathcal{S}$IBSON ·

Spaghetti Bolognese

• Serves 6 •

675 g / 1½ lb minced beef

butter for frying

450 g / 1 lb onions, chopped

¼ green pepper, deseeded and chopped

300 ml / ½ pint beef or chicken stock

225 g / 8 oz mushrooms, sliced

1 (397-g / 14-oz) can chopped tomatoes

1 tablespoon concentrated tomato purée

a few drops of Worcestershire sauce

salt and black pepper

spaghetti

Gently fry the mince in a knob of butter in a large pan. At the same time fry in another pan, also in butter, the onions and green pepper. When the meat has browned, add the stock, onions and peppers. Add mushrooms, tomatoes, tomato purée and Worcestershire sauce and stir well to combine. Add salt and pepper to taste. Cook for 35 to 40 minutes. Add thickening if necessary.

Cook the spaghetti in boiling salted water until tender.

• **Obtained by Adam Cole** •

Mexican Mince

• Serves 4 •

175 g/6 oz onions

50 g/2 oz butter

450 g/1 lb lean minced beef

1 (397-g/14-oz) can chopped tomatoes

2 tablespoons concentrated tomato purée

2 teaspoons chopped parsley

generous pinch of oregano

1 clove garlic, crushed

½ glass wine or sherry

100 g/4 oz celery, chopped

50 g/2 oz green or red peppers, deseeded and chopped

3 tablespoons mayonnaise

150 ml/¼ pint water

4 teaspoons Tabasco sauce

175 g/6 oz cooked rice

salt and pepper

a small packet of salt and vinegar crisps

Fry the onions for a few minutes in half the butter, then add the beef. After the mince has browned, add the tomatoes, tomato purée, herbs, garlic and wine or sherry. Cook until tender. Fry the celery and peppers in the remaining butter for a few minutes. Combine the mayonnaise, water and Tabasco sauce, celery, peppers, mince and rice. Season to taste with salt and pepper. Place in a large ovenproof dish.

Cook for 45 minutes in a moderate oven (180 C, 350 F, gas 4). Crush the crisps over the top and replace in the oven for 5 minutes to crisp.

• Contributed by Olive Wells •
TTTE RAF Cottesmore

Chilli con Carne

• Serves 4–6 •

675 g / 1½ lb minced beef

1 tablespoon fat or oil

1 large onion, finely chopped

1 green pepper, deseeded and chopped

1 (397-g / 14-oz) can chopped tomatoes

salt and pepper

1–2 teaspoons chilli powder, according to taste

1 tablespoon vinegar

1 teaspoon sugar

2 tablespoons concentrated tomato purée

1 (425-g / 15-oz) can red kidney beans

Fry the minced beef in the oil until lightly browned. Add the onion and pepper and fry for 5 minutes until soft. Stir in the tomatoes and add seasoning and chilli powder blended with the vinegar, sugar and tomato purée. Cover and simmer for 30 to 40 minutes. Add the kidney beans 10 minutes before the cooking time is completed.

Note

American chilli powder is the best type to use as it is generally a milder seasoning, based on Mexican ground chilli peppers.

Peasant Beef

• Serves 4 •

2 large onions, chopped

1 clove garlic, chopped

a little oil for frying

450 g / 1 lb minced beef

1 (397-g / 14-oz) can chopped tomatoes

2 tablespoons concentrated tomato purée

1 green pepper, deseeded and chopped

225 g / 8 oz mushrooms, sliced

1 large bay leaf

salt and pepper

Fry the onion and garlic in a little oil until soft and golden, then add the minced beef and brown. Add the tomatoes, tomato purée, green pepper, mushrooms, bay leaf and seasoning. Let it bubble well and then simmer until rich and red – about 45 minutes. Remove the bay leaf before serving. Serve with boiled rice and a green salad.

• **Contributed by Judy Thorpe** •
TTTE RAF Cottesmore

◆ TOMMY CANNON ◆

◆ CLIFF RICHARD ◆

Beef Curry

• Serves 3–4 •

450 g / 1 lb braising steak

a little oil

1 onion, sliced

salt and pepper

6 tablespoons water

½ teaspoon ground ginger

½ teaspoon chilli powder

4 teaspoons curry powder

1 tablespoon concentrated tomato purée

1 clove garlic, crushed

1 teaspoon cornflour

6 tablespoons milk

Cut the steak into cubes and fry in a little oil with the sliced onion, salt and pepper until the meat is brown. Add the water, ginger, chilli, curry powder, tomato purée and garlic. Simmer until the meat is tender and the liquid has thickened. Add the cornflour mixed with the milk and simmer for 20 minutes. Serve with rice and pappadums.

' For your recipe book, with best wishes. '

Beef Curry

• Serves 2–3 •

2 medium onions

50 g / 2 oz fat

2 tablespoons curry powder

½ teaspoon salt

250 ml / 8 fl oz water or beef stock

450 g / 1 lb blade of beef

Slice the onions and fry to golden brown in the fat. Mix the curry powder and salt in the water or stock. Add to the onion and stir frequently over a low heat for 30 minutes. Cut the meat into small cubes and add to the mixture. Cook until meat is tender, about 1 to 1¼ hours, adding more liquid if necessary.

• Obtained by Caroline Lilley •

The Rt Hon
NEIL
KINNOCK
MP

Rogan Josh

• **Serves 6** •

This is just an introduction –
an Indian family will have its own
combination of spices. If you add
more chilli powder, it will be hotter
– but it's up to you. Most of these
spices can now be found in
supermarkets. If you can't find
them all don't worry – but don't
forget the yogurt.

6 tablespoons oil
....
450 g/1 lb chopped onions
....
2 cloves garlic, crushed
....
1 kg/2 lb chuck steak or lean lamb, cubed
....
5 cm/2 in fresh root ginger, peeled and
crushed or finely chopped
....
1 teaspoon ground coriander
....
½ teaspoon ground cinnamon
....
½ teaspoon ground cumin
....
1 teaspoon turmeric
....
¼ teaspoon chilli powder
....
6 tablespoons natural yogurt
....
1 small can chopped tomatoes

Heat the oil and fry the onions and garlic
until slightly browned. Add the meat and
brown. Remove the onions and meat from
the pan. Cook the crushed ginger, coriander, cinnamon, cumin, turmeric and chilli
powder for about 30 seconds then add the
meat, onions, yogurt and tomatoes. Cook in
a moderate oven (180 C, 350 F, gas 4) for
about 1 hour or until the meat is tender.
Serve with plain boiled rice, poppadums,
chapati or naan bread, mango chutney and
a green vegetable salad.

❛ **Thank you for writing
to me and I do hope this
helps you in your fund
raising to help Leukaemia
Research. Best wishes
with your book.** ❜

Veal Valentino

• **Serves 4–6** •

100 g/4 oz butter
....
4–6 veal escalopes
....
150 ml/¼ pint veal or chicken stock
....
2 teaspoons flour
....
300 ml/½ pint single cream
....
salt and freshly ground pepper
....
50 g/2 oz mushrooms, sliced
....
squeeze of lemon juice
....
12 cooked asparagus spears
....
2 tablespoons grated Parmesan cheese

Melt half the butter and cook the escalopes for 6 to 7 minutes, until evenly browned on both sides. Take out of the pan and keep warm. Deglaze the pan with the stock, boil up and strain and keep. Melt 15 g/½ oz butter, carefully blend in the flour and cook for 1 to 2 minutes. Add the strained stock and cream and season, then bring to the boil, stirring constantly. Return the escalopes to the pan.

In another pan, cook the mushrooms in the remaining butter with a squeeze of lemon, add the asparagus and warm through, then add to the escalopes. Cook gently for 7 to 8 minutes. Transfer to a hot entrée dish, coat with the sauce, sprinkle over the grated cheese and brown in a hot oven (220 C, 425 F, gas 7) or under the grill. Serve with parsley potatoes.

• **Contributed by Elizabeth Swain** •
TTTE RAF Cottesmore

◆ P*ETER* W*HEELER* ◆

Loin of Lamb and Apricots

• **Serves 6** •

1.5 kg/3½ lb boned loin of lamb
....
24 cloves
....
1 (376-g/13¼-oz) can Homepride Red Wine Cook-in-Sauce
....
1 (540-g/1 lb-3-oz) can apricot halves
....
sprig of watercress to garnish

Tie the lamb securely with string and score the surface with a sharp knife. Press in the cloves at intervals along the surface of the lamb. Place in a deep casserole dish and pour over the Red Wine Cook-in-Sauce. Cover and bake in a moderate oven (180 C, 350 F, gas 4) for 1½ hours, basting the joint frequently with the sauce. Remove the lid 30 minutes before the end of the cooking time. Drain the apricots. Transfer the lamb to a warmed serving dish, pouring any remaining sauce on top. Arrange the apricots with the lamb and garnish with watercress. Serve immediately with a crisp, mixed salad.

The Rt Hon Dr
DAVID OWEN
MP

Lambs' Kidneys Cooked in Butter and Mustard Sauce

‹ I am happy to enclose one of my favourite recipes . . . I wish you every success in this fund-raising venture. I personally give a lot of support to the Leukaemia Research Organisation. ›

• Serves 2 •

knob of butter

6 lambs' kidneys

1 tablespoon finely chopped spring onions or ordinary onions

4 tablespoons dry white wine

1 tablespoon Dijon mustard

1 tablespoon butter

salt and pepper

chopped parsley to garnish

Melt a knob of butter in a shallow casserole or deep frying pan. Add the kidneys (after removing the outer skin and white fat). Cook on both sides for about 10 minutes by which time the kidneys should be cooked on the outside and pink in the centre. Remove the kidneys to a warm plate.

Add the onions to the butter in the casserole or pan and cook for 1 minute. Then add the white wine and boil, while scraping up the bits on the bottom of the casserole or pan. Take off the heat then add the mustard and tablespoon of butter along with salt and pepper to taste.

Now slice the kidneys, about 5 mm/¼ in thick, and add to the casserole. Heat over a low heat for a couple of minutes to heat the kidneys through. Add a sprinkle of parsley to garnish then serve with boiled rice.

• **Obtained by Mr P J Shelton** •

Roast Garlic Lamb

1 leg of lamb
....
3–4 cloves garlic, slivered

Prepare the lamb the night before by making incisions in the lamb and inserting the garlic slivers. The following day roast the lamb in a hot oven (220 C, 425 F, gas 7) for 15 minutes per 450 g/1 lb plus 20 minutes extra.

• **Obtained by Mr P J Shelton** •

Pork Casserole

• **Serves 3–4** •

450 g/1 lb pork fillet or tenderloin, cut into slices
....
50 g/2 oz flour and curry powder mixed together
....
salt and pepper
....
50 g/2 oz butter
....
2 onions, chopped
....
1 large leek, washed and sliced
....
100 g/4 oz celery, sliced
....
1 small green pepper, deseeded and sliced
....
1 (397-g/14-oz) can chopped tomatoes
....
2 tablespoons white wine
....
100 g/4 oz mushrooms, sliced

Coat the slices of pork in the flour, curry powder and salt and pepper. Melt the butter and fry the pork until golden brown. Remove and place in a casserole dish. Add all the other ingredients, cover and cook for about 45 minutes in a moderate oven (180 C, 350 F, gas 4).

• **Obtained by Mr P J Shelton** •

Sweet and Sour Pork

• **Serves 6–8** •

1 kg/2 lb boneless pork, cut into small pieces

25 g/1 oz flour

6 tablespoons oil

1 clove garlic, crushed

1 (425-g/15-oz) can pineapple chunks

2 green peppers, deseeded and sliced

2 red peppers, deseeded and sliced

3 tart eating apples, cored and cut into small pieces

1 (269-g/9½-oz) can bean sprouts

1 (269-g/9½-oz) can bamboo shoots

1 (269-g/9½-oz) can water chestnuts

salt and pepper

Sauce

2 tablespoons cornflour

4 tablespoons sugar

300 ml/ ½ pint chicken stock

300 ml/½ pint pineapple juice

2 tablespoons soy sauce

6 tablespoons vinegar

Coat the pork pieces with the flour. Fry the pork in the oil with the garlic until brown. Lower the heat and add the pineapple, peppers and apple. Cook until tender.

For the sauce, blend all the ingredients in a basin then pour into a saucepan, bring to the boil and cook for 3 minutes. Stir until clear. Pour over the meat and leave to simmer until cooked. For the last 10 minutes add the bean sprouts, bamboo shoots and water chestnuts. Season to taste before serving.

• **Contributed by Pat Middleton** •
TTTE RAF Cottesmore

Pork Fillets in White Wine, Mushroom and Cream Sauce

• Serves 4 •

2 (275-g/10-oz) pork fillets, cut through the middle to make 4 very thin pieces

1 tablespoon seasoned flour

50 g/2 oz butter

2 tablespoons olive oil

Sauce

225 g/8 oz mushrooms, thinly sliced

50 g/2 oz butter

1 tablespoon oil

1 tablespoon flour

6 tablespoons chicken stock

6 tablespoons dry white wine

pinch each of freshly grated nutmeg, salt and ground black pepper

1 tablespoon cream

Beat the 4 fillets until flat and thin. Toss in the seasoned flour and fry gently in the butter and oil until golden. Remove from the pan and keep warm.

To make the sauce, fry the mushrooms in the butter and oil. Add the flour then gradually add the stock, wine and seasonings. Bring to the boil, stirring continuously, and cook gently for 2 to 3 minutes. Add the pork fillets and continue to simmer gently until the meat is cooked. (Alternatively, put in an ovenproof dish in a moderate oven (180 C, 350 F, gas 4) for 30 minutes, which makes the meat very tender.) Remove from the heat or oven and add the cream just before serving.

Serve with sautéd potatoes and green vegetables or salad. The pork fillets can be substituted by chicken pieces, using exactly the same recipe.

Contributed by
• The Rt Hon Michael Latham, MP •
Obtained by Mr PJ Shelton

Somerset Pork

• **Serves 6–8** •

1.5 kg/3 lb pork steaks, beaten

25 g/1 oz butter

225 g/8 oz onions, sliced

175 g/6 oz celery, sliced

2 tablespoons flour

300 ml/½ pint dry cider

300 ml/½ pint stock

about 50 g/2 oz each of raisins, brown sugar and chopped parsley

Fry the pork in the butter, remove and keep warm. Fry the onions and celery until just soft, add the flour, cider and stock to make a smooth sauce. Pour over the pork, add the raisins, sugar and chopped parsley. Cook in a moderately hot oven (200 C, 400 F, gas 6) until pork is tender, about 50 minutes.

• **Contributed by Olive Wells** •
TTTE RAF Cottesmore

◆ *J*AMES *H*ERRIOT ◆

Panacalty

• **Serves 2** •

3 large potatoes, thinly sliced

225 g/8 oz bacon

1 large onion, sliced or chopped

salt and pepper

Put thinly sliced potatoes into a frying pan with a few drops of water, then a layer of bacon followed by a layer of onion. Continue until all the ingredients are used up. Add 300 ml/½ pint water. Season and cover. Cook until the potatoes are tender.

• **Obtained by Samantha Lilley** •

JEAN ALEXANDER
'Hilda Ogden'

Roast Ham

• **Cooking time** •
20 minutes per 450 g / 1 lb
plus 20 minutes extra

1 ham joint
....
prepared English mustard
....
brown sugar
....
cloves

Place the ham in cold water in a large saucepan and bring to the boil, simmer for a third of the total cooking time. Remove from the pan, strip off the rind and score the fat criss-cross. Spread the fat with mustard and press on a thick layer of sugar and stick with cloves. Place the ham, fat-side upper-most, in a lightly oiled roasting tin and cook in a moderately hot oven (190 C, 375 F, gas 5) for the remainder of the cooking time.

• **Obtained by Emma Smith** •

Gammon in Cider with Egg Sauce

• **Serves 6** •

1 gammon joint
....
300 ml / ½ pint cider
....
bay leaf
....
10 black peppercorns
....
Glaze
....
brown sugar
....
mustard powder
....
honey
....
Sauce
....
2 eggs
....
100 g / 4 oz sugar
....
5 tablespoons tarragon vinegar
....
150 ml / ¼ pint double cream, lightly whipped
....
1 tablespoon chopped parsley

Cook the gammon in a large saucepan with the cider, bay leaf, peppercorns and sufficient water to cover for 20 minutes per 450 g / 1 lb. Remove from the pan, take off the skin and rub in the glaze. Bake in a moderately hot oven (190 C, 375 F, gas 5) for 30 minutes.

• **Contributed by Olive Wells** •
TTTE RAF Cottesmore

Tony Wadsworth

Chow Fang

• Serves 2–4 •

400 g/14 oz Basmati rice

lard or oil for frying

1 bunch spring onions

100 g/4 oz peeled cooked prawns

4 rashers smoked back bacon

2 eggs

50 g/2 oz frozen peas

❝ Serves a couple of big 'uns and two little 'uns . . . AH-SO! Every success with the venture and kind regards to Oliver. ❞

Boil the rice for 5 to 8 minutes, until the centre is still slightly hard. Fry rice in a little lard or oil in a large frying pan. Put in a large casserole dish in a warm oven. Chop up the tops of the spring onions (keeping the actual spring onions for another dish) and fry in a pan with the prawns. Mix in with the rice in the dish in the oven. Cut up the bacon into small pieces and fry. Put into the rice mixture. Place the eggs in a cup and break the yolks and mix into the white and fry gently. Chop it all up and put into rice mixture. Boil the peas for 5 minutes and add to the mixture. Mix everything well in together.

• Obtained by Jill Bentley •

VEGETABLES

Chinese Braised Vegetables

• Serves 2–3 •

3 sticks celery, diced

2 large carrots, sliced lengthways

1 green pepper, deseeded and chopped

1 small onion, cut into fine rings

1 small cauliflower, broken into small sprigs

½ cucumber, peeled and diced

100 g/4 oz mushrooms, sliced

2 tablespoons vegetable oil

6 tablespoons water

2 teaspoons soy sauce

bean sprouts (optional)

Cook all the vegetables in the oil in a very large pan or wok for a few minutes. Add the water and the soy sauce and cook for 6 to 8 minutes, stirring occasionally. The vegetables should be crisp and crunchy. Bean sprouts may be added at the last minute.

• Contributed by Jan Creedy •

Skirly Tomatoes

• Serves 6 •

6 large, firm tomatoes

1 onion, finely chopped

½ finely chopped leek

a little butter

50 g/2 oz pinhead oatmeal

salt and pepper

pinch of freshly grated nutmeg

Cut the top third off the tomatoes and reserve. Sweat the onion and leek in a little butter until transparent. Add the oatmeal, seasonings and 4 tablespoons water. Cook until the water is absorbed. Use this mixture to stuff the tomatoes. Put the lids back on and bake in a moderate oven (180 C, 350 F, gas 4) for 20 minutes. Serve hot with steaks, chops, etc.

• Contributed by Fiona Lockwood •
TTTE RAF Cottesmore

DAVID BELLAMY

Ratatouille

- **Serves 4 normal-sized human beings, 2 Bellamies or 1 Lenny Henry** •

2 large Spanish onions

450 g/1 lb tomatoes

6 courgettes

4 small aubergines

1 green pepper

1 red pepper

2 tablespoons olive oil

2 cloves garlic, crushed

sprig of thyme

2 bay leaves

2 cups of red wine

salt and pepper

chopped parsley and tarragon to garnish

Peel, chop and slice all the vegetables or cut into chunks. Remember to remove and discard the pepper seeds, and aubergine stalks. Heat the oil in a large, strong pan and gently fry the onions and garlic. Add the vegetables, herbs and 1 cup of red wine. Season well to taste. Simmer in a pan with a well-fitting lid, simmer slowly until the vegetables are tender. After removal from the heat pour in the last cup of wine. Serve in a casserole, garnished with chopped parsley and tarragon.

❛ **Don't let your mouth water too much, and don't drink too much while you are cooking it!** ❜

Contributed by

Blue Peter, BBC

Saucy Leeks

• **Serves 2–4** •

4 large leeks

4 slices ham

25 g/1 oz butter or margarine

25 g/1 oz plain flour

150 ml/¼ pint leek stock

150 ml/¼ pint milk

75 g/3 oz cheese, grated

2 tablespoons white breadcrumbs

salt and pepper to taste

Prepare the leeks by trimming the tops and the roots from the bottom, making sure that all the dirt is out. Don't cut them up to wash them as you need to keep their shape. Wash the trimmed leeks under a running cold water tap and swish them about until every speck of dirt is gone. When they're all clean, cook them in slightly salted water for about 12 minutes until they're soft and tender. Then, when the water has cooled down, lift each leek out and put them on a piece of kitchen roll, saving the water you've cooked them in for the sauce. Dry the leeks off, either with a piece of kitchen roll, or squeeze the excess water out with a spoon and now they're ready to parcel up.

Wrap one thin slice of ham round each leek. Arrange the parcelled-up leeks in an oven-proof dish with the fold at the *bottom* and put them on one side while you make the sauce.

For the white sauce, melt the butter or margarine over a low heat and then add the flour. Stir them together instantly, and keep stirring until the mixture is smooth, with no lumps, until it's well cooked, but *not* burnt. You should stir for at least a minute. When it's cooked, you can add the liquid, a mixture of the milk and the same amount of the water you cooked the leeks in. **Keep stirring** – if you don't, the mixture will go lumpy. Turn the heat up slowly, and bring the whole mixture gently to the boil. It will bubble when it boils, but don't stop stirring for at least a minute after that. When it's cooked it should be perfectly smooth. Now add the cheese flavouring. Use two-thirds of your cheese – the remainder you'll need for the topping. Stir it very well to spread it around – the whole secret of this recipe is thorough stirring. When it's all blended together, pour it over the top of the leeks and ham, so they are evenly covered and smooth it with a spoon if necessary. The final touch is to sprinkle the rest of the grated cheese over the top, plus the breadcrumbs – this adds a nice crunch to the sauce.

Cook the leeks and ham in a moderately hot oven (200 C, 400 F, gas 6) for 30 minutes, or until the top is crisp and brown. This recipe is sufficient for a meal for two, or a snack for four people. Crusty bread goes well with this recipe to dip into the sauce.

Fried Aubergine

• Serves 4 •

1 kg/2 lb aubergines, sliced and salted
....
5 tablespoons olive oil
....
2 tablespoons wine vinegar
....
½ teaspoon finely chopped garlic
....
3 anchovies
....
pinch of oregano

Fry the aubergines in the oil but do not brown. Dry on kitchen paper. In a small pan mix the olive oil, vinegar, garlic, anchovies and oregano together. Boil for 3 minutes. Serve on a dish in alternate layers of aubergine and sauce.

• **Contributed by Enrica Chiavolini** •
TTTE RAF Cottesmore

MARQUESS OF TAVISTOCK

Cauliflower Soufflé au Gratin

• Serves 2–3 •

1 large cauliflower
....
40 g/1½ oz butter
....
40 g/1½ oz flour
....
600 ml/1 pint milk
....
225 g/8 oz Cheddar cheese, grated
....
3 eggs, separated
....
salt and pepper
....
25 g/1 oz breadcrumbs

Cut the cauliflower into tiny florets, place in a saucepan, cover with water and bring to the boil, strain and keep warm. Melt the butter, stir in the flour and cook for 2 minutes then add the milk and bring slowly to the boil until thick. Stir in 175 g/6 oz of the cheese and the egg yolks. Season with salt and pepper. Whisk the egg whites until stiff. Stir the cauliflower into the sauce, fold in the egg whites and pour into a greased 1.75-litres/3-pints soufflé dish. Sprinkle on a layer of cheese then a layer of bread-crumbs, then the rest of the cheese, this ensures a crispy topping. Bake for 25 to 30 minutes in a moderately hot oven (190 C, 375 F, gas 5) and serve immediately.

ℒES ⅅAWSON

' Delicious! '

Spud

Bake one potato in its jacket for 20 minutes in a hot oven (220 C, 425 F, gas 7). Remove from the oven. Take out middle of potato with an apple corer and cram with butter, herbs and black pepper and seal potato. Put back in oven for another 20 minutes.

Gratin Dauphinois

• Serves 4 •

450 g / 1 lb potatoes
....
40 g / 1½ oz butter
....
1 clove garlic, crushed
....
salt and pepper
....
150 ml / ¼ pint double cream
....
150 ml / ¼ pint milk

Peel and slice the potatoes. Then in a well buttered gratin dish, arrange a layer of potato slices, sprinkle with the crushed garlic, salt and pepper. Add another layer of potatoes and season again. Now mix cream and milk, pour over the potatoes and add flecks of butter. Bake for 1 hour in a moderately hot oven (190 C, 375 F, gas 5).

Contributed by
• **Colonel T C S Haywood** •

Greek Dish Starter

• Serves 4 •

450 g / 1 lb cooked leeks, cut small
....
2 medium potatoes, cooked
....
225 g / 8 oz strong cheese, grated
....
3 eggs, beaten well together
....
salt and pepper to taste
....
2 tablespoons vegetable oil

Mix together the leeks, potatoes, 200 g / 7 oz cheese, 2 beaten eggs and seasoning in a large bowl. Put 1 tablespoon vegetable oil in a meat dish. Add the mixture to the dish. Put 1 tablespoon of oil on top and the reserved beaten egg and cheese to cover the top. Cook in a moderately hot oven (190 C, 375 F, gas 5) for 35 minutes.

• **Contributed by Peggy Corry** •

· SAVOURIES ·

Risotto with Saffron

• Serves 6 •

½ Spanish onion

100 g / 4 oz unsalted butter

450 g / 1 lb brown 'Easy-cook' rice

1.15 litres / 2 pints stock

salt and pepper

¼ teaspoon saffron powder

100 g / 4 oz Parmesan Cheese, grated

Slice the onion thinly, put into a saucepan with the butter and cook till brown. Add the rice and stir with a wooden spoon so that it doesn't stick. Gradually stir in the stock with a little salt and pepper. Dissolve the saffron in a little stock and add to the rice after 10 minutes of cooking. Cook for another 10 minutes. Serve with a little butter and the Parmesan cheese.

• Contributed by Anna Missarino •

Sausage and Tomato Quiche

• Serves 6 •

225 g/8 oz chipolata sausages

75 g/3 oz Cheddar cheese, grated

2 tomatoes, peeled and sliced

2 eggs

250 ml/8 fl oz milk

½ teaspoon dried basil

salt and pepper

Shortcrust Pastry

175 g/6 oz plain flour

100 g/4 oz butter or margarine

2 tablespoons cold water

Make the pastry by rubbing the flour and fat together until the mixture resembles fine breadcrumbs. Mix in the water to form a dough.

Grill the sausages until lightly browned. Line a 23-cm/9-in flan dish with the pastry. Prick the base and sides with a fork and bake blind for 20 minutes in a moderately hot oven (200 C, 400 F, gas 6). Sprinkle the cheese over the base of the cooked pastry case. Arrange the cooked sausages in a wheel design. Put the tomato slices in the spaces. Beat the eggs, stir in the milk, add the basil and season with salt and pepper. Pour this savoury custard over the filling. Turn the temperature down to moderate (180 C, 350 F, gas 4) and bake the quiche for 30 to 35 minutes. Serve hot or cold.

• Contributed by Mark Wallington •

Asparagus Quiche

• Serves 6 •

4 rashers bacon

1 (23-cm/9-in) cooked pastry flan case

1 (425-g/15-oz) can asparagus

2 eggs

1 tablespoon finely chopped onion

150 g/6 oz single cream or creamy milk

50 g/2 oz grated cheese, plus extra cheese for topping

salt and pepper

Cook the bacon, chop and place in the prepared pastry case. Cut the asparagus into 2.5 cm/1 in lengths and place in the case. Beat the eggs and add the onion, cream, cheese and seasoning. Pour carefully into the case. Sprinkle a little extra cheese on top. Bake in a moderately hot oven (200 C, 400 F, gas 6) for 10 minutes. Reduce the temperature to moderate (180 C, 350 F, gas 4) and continue baking for 25 to 30 minutes until the filling is set.

• Contributed by Mrs Audrey Mount •

◆ SIMON BATES ◆

Cheese Soufflé

• Serves 2–3 •

150 g/5 oz cheese, grated
....
25 g/1 oz butter
....
150 ml/¼ pint milk
....
pinch of cayenne
....
5 eggs, separated

Melt 25 g/1oz cheese and the butter in a saucepan. Add the milk and cayenne. Add egg yolks and remaining cheese to the mixture and stir off the heat. Whisk the egg whites until stiff then fold into the cheese mixture. Bake in a hot oven (220 C, 425 F, gas 7) for 20 to 25 minutes. 'Eat, jolly quickly.'

Cheese Fondue

• Serves 6 •

1 French stick
....
675 g/1½ lb cheese (Gruyère or Emmental)
....
½ clove garlic
....
600 ml/1 pint dry white wine
....
5 teaspoons lemon juice
....
salt, pepper, nutmeg
....
1 glass cherry schnapps

Cut the bread into cubes and the cheese into small pieces. Rub the inside of the fondue pot with garlic. Heat the wine and lemon juice gently. Then place cheese into the liquid and stir well, beat until the cheese is boiling. Remove the pot from the heat and add the seasoning and schnapps. The fondue should be served on a rechaud. Pick up a cube of bread and dip into the cheese. Serve with a dry white wine. Guten Appetit!

• **Contributed by Vera Hoppe** •
TTTE RAF Cottesmore

Scone-based Pizza

• **Serves 4–6** •

Base

pinch of salt and pepper

225 g/8 oz self-raising flour

100 g/4 oz margarine or butter

50–100 g/2–4 oz Leicestershire cheese, grated

1 egg

5–6 tablespoons milk

Topping

1 (397-g/14-oz) can chopped tomatoes

50 g/2 oz Leicestershire cheese

4 rashers bacon, chopped

25–50 g/1–2 oz mushrooms, sliced

1 small onion, sliced

Sift the seasoning and flour into a large mixing bowl. Rub in the margarine until the mixture resembles fine breadcrumbs. Add grated cheese. Mix with egg and milk to a dough and knead lightly. Roll out the dough to fit a shallow baking tin.

Strain the juice from the tomatoes and spread the pulp over the base. Sprinkle the grated cheese over the tomatoes. Place the chopped bacon, mushroom and onion in alternate layers over the top of the pizza. Pour half the tomato juice over the pizza. Bake in the middle of a hot oven (230 C, 450 F, gas 8) for 20 to 30 minutes.

Contributed by
• **Sister Pauline Wells** •

Zwiebel Kuchen

• **Serves 4–6** •

225 g/8 oz plain flour

15 g/½ oz fresh yeast, crumbled

250 ml/8 fl oz lukewarm milk

50 g/2 oz margarine or butter, softened

450 g/1 lb onions, chopped

100 g/4 oz bacon, chopped

6 tablespoons soured cream

2 eggs

100 g/4 oz Emmental cheese, grated

salt and pepper

1 teaspoon caraway seeds

Put the flour into a bowl, make a well in the centre and put in the yeast and 2 tablespoons of the milk. Put a little flour over and leave in a warm place for 15 minutes.

Mix the rest of the milk and the margarine in the bowl of the yeast mixture to form a dough and leave for 15 minutes.

In the meantime, lightly fry the onions and bacon. Put the yeast mixture into a greased tin. Put the bacon and onion mixture on the top.

Make a mixture of the soured cream, eggs, grated cheese, salt, pepper and caraway seeds, put on the top of the mixture in the tin. Bake in a moderately hot oven (200 C, 400 F, gas 6) for 30 to 40 minutes. Serve warm with a dry wine.

• **Contributed by Waltraut Pasch** •
TTTE RAF Cottesmore

Eggs on Top

• Enough for 4 people •

Empty a large can of tomatoes or beans or spaghetti into a saucepan and bring to the boil, then empty into a shallow dish or casserole. Break 4 eggs on top then cover with grated cheese and cook under grill until cheese is melted and eggs are cooked. Serve with French fries or French bread.

• Contributed by Kathy Staff •

Duke of Buccleuch & Queensberry

Egg Cutlets

• Serves 2–3 •

25 g/1 oz butter

25 g/1 oz flour

150 ml/¼ pint milk

salt and pepper

3 hard-boiled eggs, finely chopped

flour to coat

beaten egg

breadcrumbs

butter for frying

Melt the butter, add the flour then the milk to make a white sauce. Season and add finely chopped eggs. Let get thoroughly cold. Shape into cutlets. Flour then dip in egg and breadcrumbs. Shallow fry in butter until golden brown on each side.

Contributed by

Lady Boardman

Mushroom Roulade

• Serves 4 •

50 g/2 oz butter

50 g/2 oz flour

pinch of salt

450 ml/¾ pint milk

4 eggs, separated

1 teaspoon sugar

finely toasted breadcrumbs to coat

2 medium onions, finely chopped

3 tablespoons olive oil

450 g/1 lb mushrooms, finely chopped

2 tablespoons lemon juice

2 tablespoons chopped pimento

3 tablespoons soured cream and chopped chives to serve

Line a large baking tin with Bakewell paper, dust lightly with flour, if other paper is used grease it. In a saucepan melt the butter, stir in the flour and a pinch of salt and cook the roux over a medium heat, stirring for several minutes. Gradually beat in the milk and cook the sauce, stirring constantly until it is smooth and very thick. Remove the pan from the heat and stir in the egg yolks and 1 teaspoon sugar, cool mixture. Whisk the egg whites stiffly and fold into the mixture. Spread the batter evenly over the prepared tin and bake in a moderate oven (160 C, 325 F, gas 3) for 40 or 45 minutes until it is golden and pulls away from the sides of the pan. Invert the tin over two overlapping sheets of Bakewell paper sprinkled with fine toasted breadcrumbs, lift off the tin and peel the paper from the bottom.

Make the filling, sauté the onions in the olive oil until they are tender and golden. Add the mushrooms and cook the mixture over low heat, stirring frequently until it is dry in texture. Remove the mushroom mixture from the heat and stir in the lemon juice and chopped pimento. Season with salt and pepper to taste.

Spread the roll with mushroom filling and roll it up with the aid of the paper, lifting and rolling it gently into itself. Serve the roll hot with lightly salted soured cream mixed with chopped chives.

Macaroni and Cheese

• Serves 3–4 •

225 g/8 oz macaroni
....
1 teaspoon butter
....
1 egg, beaten
....
1 teaspoon mustard powder
....
1 teaspoon salt
....
250 ml/8 fl oz milk
....
100 g/4 oz Cheddar cheese, grated

Boil the macaroni in water until tender and drain thoroughly. Stir in the butter and egg. Mix together the mustard powder and salt with 1 tablespoon hot water and add to the milk. Add the cheese, leaving a little on one side to sprinkle on top. Pour into a buttered casserole, add the milk mixture, sprinkle with the reserved cheese. Bake in a moderate oven (180 C, 350 F, gas 4) for about 45 minutes or until the custard is set and the top is crusty.

• Obtained by Victoria Rose •

Penne alla Vodka

• Serves 4 •

½ onion, thinly sliced
....
olive oil for frying
....
150 g/5 oz ham, diced
....
2 small glasses vodka
....
450 g/1 lb peeled tomatoes
....
salt to taste
....
450 g/1 lb 'Penne' pasta (quills)
....
300 ml/½ pint double cream

Brown the onion in the oil, then add the diced ham and pour out one small glass of vodka. Let the vodka evaporate, then add the peeled tomatoes and salt. Leave to cook over a low heat while you prepare the pasta. Cook the pasta for about 10 minutes. Do not overcook the pasta, then drain. Put together the pasta, sauce, double cream and remaining vodka in a pan and amalgamate for 2 to 3 minutes then serve hot.

• Contributed by Viviana Francini •
TTTE RAF Cottesmore

Penne al Salmone

• Serves 6 •

50 g/2 oz butter
....
1 tablespoon oil
....
1 (439-g/15½-oz) can salmon
....
225 g/8 oz peas
....
1 tablespoon chopped parsley
....
pinch of salt
....
450 g/1 lb 'Penne' pasta (quills)

Fry slightly the butter and oil together. When they are brown add the salmon and peas, then add the parsley and salt. Cook the 'Penne' pasta in plenty of lightly salted water, strain the pasta and add to the salmon and peas.

• **Contributed by Maria Grazia Tubi** •
TTTE RAF Cottesmore

Red Spaghetti

• Serves 4 •

8 medium tomatoes
....
3 cloves garlic
....
1 chilli
....
oil for frying
....
salt
....
450 g/1 lb spaghetti or other pasta
....
chopped parsley
....
50 g/2 oz Parmesan cheese, grated

Peel and remove the seeds from the tomatoes. Chop the garlic and chilli and fry in oil for 5 minutes. Add tomatoes, stir well and fry for another 15 minutes. Add salt to taste. While the sauce is frying, boil a pan of water: when boiling add the salt and pasta. Boil for 15 to 20 minutes. Serve the spaghetti with the sauce, plenty of parsley and grated Parmesan cheese.

• **Contributed by Ama Di Renzo** •
TTTE RAF Cottesmore

· SEBASTIAN COE ·

Spaghetti alla Carbonara

• Serves 4–6 •

450 g/1 lb spaghetti

100 g/4 oz rindless streaky bacon, chopped

4 eggs

2 teaspoons single cream

50 g/2 oz Parmesan cheese, grated

ground black pepper

‘ I have great pleasure in enclosing my favourite recipe for your Recipe Book. I hope that it will be suitable and that your project is a great success. ’

Cook the spaghetti in a large saucepan of boiling water for about 8 minutes, until tender but still firm (*al dente*).

Meanwhile, fry the bacon in its own fat until crisp. Beat the eggs in a bowl and add the cream and half the cheese. Season with the black pepper. Drain the cooked spaghetti and return it to the pan. Quickly stir in the bacon. Immediately add the egg mixture and toss well together. (The heat of the spaghetti will be enough to cook the eggs.) Serve at once, sprinkled with the remaining cheese.

> ❛ Thank you very much for asking me to contribute to your recipe book in aid of Leukaemia Research. It is a wonderful idea and I'm sure it will prove a worthy fund-raiser. ❜

Spaghetti alla Carbonara

• Serves 4 •

450 g / 1 lb spaghetti

5 rashers bacon

2 egg yolks

2 tablespoons chopped chives

250 ml / 8 fl oz cream

salt and freshly ground black pepper

1 clove garlic, crushed

grated Parmesan cheese and chopped chives to serve

Cook the spaghetti in boiling, salted water for about 10 minutes. Fry or grill the bacon until crisp, drain off the fat and break into pieces.

Beat the egg yolks, chives and cream together then add the bacon. Season, if necessary, and heat the mixture in a double boiler (or in a bowl over a pan of hot water). It's ready when thick enough to coat the back of a spoon.

Add the crushed garlic and then strain the spaghetti and thoroughly mix in the bacon sauce. Serve with grated Parmesan cheese and chopped chives.

Spaghetti Ragoût

• Serves 2 •

225 g / 8 oz onions

50 g / 2 oz butter

salt and pepper

pinch of sage or mixed herbs

75 g / 3 oz long spaghetti

2 (397-g / 14-oz) cans peeled tomatoes

175 g / 6 oz strong-flavoured Cheddar cheese

sprigs of parsley to garnish

Peel and slice the onions and fry in the melted butter until tender and golden brown. Arrange in an ovenproof dish and season with salt, pepper and herbs. Break the spaghetti into 7.5 cm / 3 in lengths and scatter over the top of the onion. Pour the tomatoes over to cover the spaghetti and arrange the grated cheese in an even layer over the top. Cover with kitchen foil or lid and bake in a cool oven (150 C, 300 F, gas 2) for 1¾ hours. Remove foil or lid and return to moderately hot oven (190 C, 375 F, gas 5) for 10 to 15 minutes, or until golden brown. Garnish with parsley sprigs and serve at once.

Spicy Spaghetti

• Serves 4 •

225 g / 8 oz wholemeal spaghetti

4 tablespoons olive oil

2–3 cloves garlic, crushed

2–3 chillies, deseeded and finely chopped

salt and freshly ground pepper

Cook the spaghetti in boiling salted water until it is *al dente* (still firm and definitely *not* soggy). While it is cooking heat up some olive oil in a frying pan and put in the garlic and chilli. Cook these very gently so they stay tender and don't get frizzled up.

When the spaghetti is done, empty it into a colander and allow to steam dry for a moment. Then put it back in the empty pan and pour over the hot olive oil, garlic and chilli. Season with black pepper.

Contributed by

Blue Peter, BBC

Sausage Risotto

• Serves 4 •

1 medium onion, sliced

1 tablespoon oil or dripping

2 rashers rindless streaky bacon, cut into small pieces

8 chipolata sausages

100 g/4 oz long-grain rice

salt and pepper

1 (227-g/8-oz) can tomatoes

25–50 g/1–2 oz Cheddar cheese, grated

Peel and slice the onion and fry it gently in a tablespoon of oil or dripping for about 5 minutes, until it's soft and golden brown. Remove the onions and set aside for later.

Put the bacon into the frying pan. Prick the chipolata sausages so they don't burst and then fry them with the bacon for about 10 minutes until cooked. Whilst the bacon and sausages are cooking put the rice into boiling lightly salted water and cook for 10 minutes. When the bacon and sausages are cooked remove the pan from the heat and cut each sausage into 3 or 4 pieces. Put the pan back on the heat. Add the tomatoes and the onions, then add salt and ground black pepper to taste. Stir the mixture well until it's all heated through. Turn off the heat and add the rice which should now be cooked and the cheese. (Vary the amount of cheese according to how strong you want the flavour to be.) Stir everything well and then tip the risotto into a serving dish. Serve immediately.

Savoury Snack

• Serves 1–2 •

butter for spreading
....
2–4 slices of bread
....
4 peeled tomatoes, sliced
....
salt and pepper
....
½–1 teaspoon dried mixed herbs
....
100–225 g/4–8 oz cheese, grated
....
8 slices bacon

Thickly butter the bread then place on a greased tray. Cover the bread thickly with the sliced tomatoes. Season and sprinkle with herbs. Place the grated cheese on top and make lattice pattern with the bacon. Cook for 25 minutes in a moderately hot oven (200 C, 400 F, gas 6).

• **Contributed by Mrs Jennie Fox** •

Supper Dish for Two

• Serves 2 •

1 can creamed corn
....
4 slices ham
....
50 g/2 oz grated cheese

Spread the corn inside the ham slices, roll up and place in a greased ovenproof dish. Sprinkle with the cheese. Bake in a moderate oven (180 C, 350 F, gas 4) until the cheese has melted, about 30 minutes.

• **Contributed by Anne Major** •
TTTE RAF Cottesmore

TERRY WOGAN

Chip Butty

• Serves 1 •

2 slices of fresh white bread
....
butter
....
chips
....
salt and pepper
....
dressing (tomato ketchup or relish of choice)

Take two slices of fresh white bread. Spread liberally with butter. Fill with sizzling hot, freshly fried chips. Add seasoning and dressing to taste – EAT!!

Bacon, Cheese and Marmite Sandwiches

• Serves 1 •

butter for spreading

2 slices brown bread

Marmite

Cheddar cheese slices

grilled bacon rashers

Butter two slices of brown bread and spread *one* buttered slice only with Marmite. Cover the Marmite with slices of Cheddar cheese, then 'top' with the sizzling rashers of bacon. Place the second slice of bread on the top. Cut into quarters and serve immediately with a nice cup of tea (no sugar!).

Chappaties

• Makes 12 •

225 g/8 oz wholemeal flour

1 teaspoon salt

6 tablespoons water

melted butter

Sieve the flour and salt into a bowl. Gradually add the water and make into a dough.

Knead for 10 to 15 minutes, then leave in a warm place covered with a cloth for 30 minutes. Divide into 12 pieces. Roll each piece into thin pancakes on a floured board.

Heat a lightly greased frying pan and cook one chappati at a time. During cooking, after about 1 minute, the surface of the chappati will blister. Press down to puncture and flatten the surface. Turn the chappati over and cook the other side. Serve hot.

Contributed by
• **RAF North Luffenham** •
Officers' Mess

Labskaus

• Serves 4 •

5 small onions, diced

25 g/1 oz butter

575 g/1¼ lb corned beef, chopped

4 portions mashed potatoes

6 slices pickled beetroot, diced, and a little juice

6 small pickled cucumbers, diced

pinch each of salt, pepper, nutmeg

4 herrings or cooked eggs

In a small pan simmer the onions in a little butter, add the corned beef to warm it up. To the already hot mashed potatoes add the above mixture, then put in the beetroot, pickled cucumber, salt, pepper and nutmeg. Mix it all carefully and let it simmer for about 15 minutes. You can serve this with warm herrings or hot eggs of any kind.

• **Contributed by Angelika Boehnke** •
TTTE RAF Cottesmore

*E*AMONN
*A*NDREWS

Mystery Potato

old potatoes
....
butter
....
Filling
....
chopped onion
....
grated cheese
....
eggs
....
tinned salmon

First of all, get nice, large, old potatoes – it won't work with new ones – and scrub them as clean as a whistle but don't take off the skins. Dry the potatoes and stab them well with a fork. Whatever you do, don't forget the stabbing because if you don't prick these potatoes, you'll have a mighty explosion inside your oven and you'll not be the most popular person in the house by the time somebody has scraped off exploded potato from all round the oven. Bake the potatoes in a moderately hot oven (200 C, 400 F, gas 6).

Now you've plenty of time to think of your mystery filling. I leave the potatoes in there for an hour or so till the skin is crackling and crispy. When they're done, you'll need a cloth or oven gloves to handle them. Try and split each one down the middle. Pop a tiny blob of butter, if you're not dieting, or a drop of milk if you are, and then almost

anything you like. Sometimes I go for a spoonful or so of chopped onion, sometimes a spoonful or two of grated cheese. I've even popped an egg in there and once tried some tinned salmon which wasn't at all bad. And don't forget to eat the skins afterwards. If you get very ambitious, you can always split the baked potato right down the middle, scoop out and then refill each half.

❛ The best recipes for people like me are simple ones. This is one of my favourites because you can vary it to your heart's content and – hopefully – never grow tired of it. It's simply baking a potato and giving it a little filling. The Mystery Potato. ❜

• DESSERTS •

Lemon Layer Pudding

• Serves 4 •

grated rind and juice of 1 lemon

50 g/2 oz butter

100 g/4 oz sugar

2 eggs, separated

50 g/2 oz self-raising flour

300 ml/½ pint milk

Add the lemon rind to the butter and sugar and beat the mixture until pale and fluffy. Add the egg yolks and flour and beat well. Stir in the milk and 2 to 3 tablespoons lemon juice.

Whisk the egg whites until stiff, fold in and pour the mixture into a buttered ovenproof dish. Stand in a shallow tin of water and cook in a moderately hot oven (200 C, 400 F, gas 6) for about 45 minutes, or until the top is set and spongy to touch. This pudding will separate into a custard layer with a sponge topping.

• Contributed by Gary Linekar •

Apple and Almond Bake

• Serves 4 •

150 g/5 oz soft margarine

2 large eggs

225 g/8 oz caster sugar

225 g/8 oz self-raising flour

1½ teaspoons baking powder

½ teaspoon almond essence

350 g/12 oz sliced cooked apples

25 g/1 oz flaked almonds

Beat together the margarine, eggs, sugar, flour, baking powder and almond essence. Put half the mixture into a bowl or baking dish. Fold in the apple. Spread the remainder on top then sprinkle on the flaked almonds. Bake in a moderate oven (160 C, 325 F, gas 3) for 1½ hours. Serve with fresh cream or custard.

• Contributed by Averil Foster •
TTTE RAF Cottesmore

TORVILLE AND DEAN

Apple Crumble

• Serves 4 •

675 g/1½ lb cooking apples

1 tablespoon water

knob of butter

75 g/3 oz soft brown sugar

pinch of ground cinnamon

Topping

100 g/4 oz plain flour

75 g/3 oz butter

50 g/2 oz soft brown sugar

‘ Chris' favourite recipe is a fruit crumble, and mine is trifle. We do hope that they will be of some help with your fund raising endeavours, and wish you every possible success. ’

Peel, core and slice the apples then place in a saucepan with the water, butter, sugar and cinnamon. Cover with a lid and cook on a low heat for about 5 to 10 minutes, until the apples are tender. Place the apples in a pie or soufflé dish and leave to cool slightly.

Meanwhile, make the topping by sifting the flour into a bowl and add the butter, cut into pieces. Rub in until the mixture resembles fine breadcrumbs then add the sugar. Mix in well then place on top of the apple. Bake in a moderately hot oven (190 C, 375 F, gas 5) for 30 minutes.

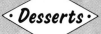

ROBIN KNOX-JOHNSON

‘ **This is very useful at sea as fresh water is usually short and salt water can be used for boiling. Best of luck with the book.** ’

Plum Duff

• Serves 1–2 •

To be made when sailing around the world!

half a mug of flour

1 teaspoon yeast

1 dessertspoon sugar

a handful of currants

water to mix

Take an enamel mug, and grease the sides with butter. Mix the flour with sufficient water to form a dough then add the yeast. Add sugar and currants. Place this gooey mess into the mug, wrap in a tea cloth and then place in a saucepan of boiling water and allow it to steam for 30 to 45 minutes.

• Obtained by Mr P J Shelton •

Country Pudding

• Serves 4 •

675 g/1½ lb cooking apples

175 g/6 oz demerara sugar

1–2 tablespoons water

120 g/4½ oz butter

175 g/6 oz rolled oats

150 ml/¼ pint double or whipping cream

grated chocolate to decorate

Cook the peeled, cored and sliced apples with 40 g/1½ oz of the sugar and the water until tender. Leave to cool. Melt the butter, add the remaining sugar and the oats. Place a layer of apples in a glass dish, cover with a layer of oat mixture. Repeat the layers, ending with the oat mixture on top. Whip the cream and place on the top. Decorate with grated chocolate.

• Contributed by Mrs Joyce Mount •

HRH
THE *P*RINCE OF
*W*ALES

Bread and Butter Pudding

• Serves 6 •

8–10 large slices bread and butter
....
50 g/2 oz currants
....
50 g/2 oz sultanas
....
50 g/2 oz raisins
....
1–2 bananas, sliced
....
black treacle
....
about 600 ml/1 pint milk
....
brandy to taste
....
ground cinnamon to sprinkle

Line a baking dish with a layer of bread and butter. Cover with currants, sultanas, raisins, sliced banana and a little black treacle. Cover with more bread and butter, currants, etc. as before and continue in layers until the top of the dish is reached. Pour in enough milk until the mixture is sufficiently wet. Pour in brandy to taste. Top with the remaining bread and butter, and sprinkle with ground cinnamon. Cook in a moderately hot oven (200 C, 400 F, gas 6) for 30 to 45 minutes, depending on how crispy you like the bread. Add lots of cream when serving.

• **Obtained by Zoe Noone** •

· Su Pollard ·

LORD Montagu OF Beaulieu

❝ Every success with your book. Kind regards. ❞

Baked Bananas

• Serves 4 •

4 bananas
....
1 lemon
....
1 orange
....
rum (if none available syrup will do)
....
brown sugar

Cut the bananas lengthways and place in an ovenproof dish. Pour the juice of the lemon over the bananas, then the orange juice. Grate the rind of the lemon and orange and sprinkle over the bananas. Cover the bananas with rum and brown sugar. (Rum is optional but does add a lovely flavour.) Bake in a moderately hot oven (200 C, 400 F, gas 6) for 20 minutes. This dish can be served with fresh cream, but is very rich so I suggest it is served on its own.

• **Obtained by Mr P J Shelton** •

Banana Flambé

• Serves 4–6 •

25 g/1 oz brown sugar
....
50 g/2 oz butter
....
white wine or Marsala
....
4–6 bananas
....
eggcupful of lime or lemon juice
....
half a wine glass of Tia Maria
....
half a wine glass of brandy

Cover the bottom of a medium-sized frying pan with the brown sugar and heat until it begins to caramelise. Add knobs of butter and some white wine or Marsala, and heat gently until there is a liquid sauce. Cut the bananas in half lengthwise and across (4 quarters) and place in the pan. Squeeze the lime or lemon juice over them. Cook slowly until they begin to soften. Add the Tia Maria. Cook for a few minutes. Finally add the brandy. Light and serve. You can serve with cream and burnt almonds, if desired.

Contributed by

Chief Constable Alan Goodson

Banana Bake

• **Serves 4** •

1 egg

150 ml / ¼ pint milk

3 slices white bread

8 small bananas

2 tablespoons lemon juice

100 g / 4 oz butter

100 g / 4 oz brown sugar

3 lemon slices to decorate

whipped cream to serve

Beat egg into the milk. Remove the crusts from the bread and peel the bananas. Arrange the bread on the bottom of an ovenproof dish, pour on the egg mixture, put the bananas on top, then pour over the lemon juice.

Melt the butter and sugar together slowly in a saucepan and cover the bread and bananas with this mixture. Bake in a moderately hot oven (200 C, 400 F, gas 6) for 20 minutes. Decorate with lemon slices and serve with whipped cream.

• **Obtained by Joanne Taylor** •

❛ **I am pleased to send you my favourite recipe, which my wife tells me is very fattening!** ❜

Contributed by

Duchess of Rutland

❛ I hope your book will be
a great success. ❜

Rum Baba

• Serves 4–6 •

1 sponge ring or savarin

2–3 tablespoons rum (to taste)

300 ml / ½ pint double or whipping cream

maraschino cherries and angelica to
decorate

Soak the sponge ring or savarin with the
rum, adding more or less rum as desired –
according to the size of the ring. Whip the
cream and use to fill the ring. Decorate the
cream with maraschino cherries and
angelica.

• **Obtained by Samantha Lilley** •

DAVID MOORCROFT

❛ Best wishes
for the book. ❜

Easy Pavlova

• Serves 4–6 •

3 egg whites

1 teaspoon vinegar

8 tablespoons sugar

1½ tablespoons cornflour

1 teaspoon vanilla essence

4 tablespoons boiling water

Beat all the ingredients together, except the
water, until thick. Add the water and beat
again until stiff. Place in a nest shape on a
greased tray on non-stick baking paper (run
the paper under cold water first). Cook in a
moderately hot oven (190 C, 375 F, gas 5)
for 5 minutes, then turn the temperature
down to very cool (110 C, 225 F, gas ¼)
and cook for 10 minutes. Turn the oven off
and leave the pavlova in the oven until cold.

• **Obtained by Mr P J Shelton** •

◆ NIGEL MANSELL ◆

❝ We wish you every success with this venture for this very excellent cause. ❞

Pavlova

• Serves 6 •

4 egg whites

225 g/8 oz caster sugar

5 teaspoons cornflour

2 teaspoons vinegar

½ teaspoon vanilla essence

150 ml/¼ pint double cream, whipped

fresh fruit to top

Whisk the egg whites until thick and creamy in consistency. Add half the amount of sugar, continuing whisking until thick and leaves a trail. Add remaining sugar, cornflour, vinegar and vanilla essence, and combine together well. Place in an oven-proof serving dish and bake in a cool oven (140 C, 275 F, gas 1) for 1½ hours. Leave to cool, serve topped with whipped cream and fresh fruit.

• Obtained by Mr P J Shelton •

Contributed by

the Bishop of Leicester

❝ I hope your book will be a great success. ❞

Real Chocolate Mousse

50 g/2 oz plain chocolate per person

1 egg per person

Separate the white from the yolk of the egg. Melt the chocolate carefully by breaking it into small pieces into a basin and keeping the basin over a saucepan of hot water. (Be careful not to get any water into the chocolate.) As it melts, stir the chocolate till it is smooth.

As soon as the chocolate is softened (don't let it get too hot) take the basin out of the pan of hot water and stir the egg yolk into the chocolate. Mix well. Whisk the egg white until it stands in stiff peaks, then add to the chocolate/egg mixture. Using a metal spoon, add a little egg white at a time and fold in gently. Don't stir too much or the stiff texture will be lost. When the mixture is smooth pour it into small individual glasses or bowls and put to set in a fridge or cool larder.

• Obtained by Juliette Turner •

Contributed by

Lady Boardman

Chocolate Pudding Roll

• Serves 8 •

225 g/8 oz plain chocolate

2 tablespoons hot water

6 eggs, separated

225 g/8 oz caster sugar

whipped cream to fill

Dissolve 175 g/6 oz of the chocolate in the water in a small bowl over a pan of simmering water, remove from the heat. Beat the egg yolks and sugar, fold into liquid chocolate mixture. Whisk the egg whites until stiff and fold into the mixture. Line a shallow, rectangular baking tin with Bakewell paper or greased greaseproof paper and pour in the mixture. Cook for 20 minutes in a moderate oven (180 C, 350 F, gas 4). Take out, cover with a damp tea-towel and leave until wanted: it will keep until the next day. Grate the rest of the chocolate. Lift the roll out of the baking tin onto a large sheet of greaseproof paper, fill with whipped cream and roll. Sprinkle the grated chocolate on top of roll to decorate.

Chocolate Rum Truffles

• Makes 36 •

100 g/4 oz plain chocolate

50 g/2 oz butter

rum to taste

2 egg yolks

25 g/1 oz ground almonds

25 g/1 oz stale cake crumbs

225 g/8 oz icing sugar, sifted

drinking chocolate

Break up the chocolate and put with the butter in a basin standing over a saucepan of hot water. Leave until both have melted, stirring occasionally. Add the rum and egg yolks. Mix in well. Work in the remaining ingredients (except the drinking chocolate). Transfer to a cool place and leave until firm (about 1½ hours). Roll equal amounts of the mixture into 36 balls. Toss in drinking chocolate. Transfer to fluted sweet paper cases.

• **Contributed by Timothy Green** •
ex Headboy

Frozen Chocolate and Coffee Mousse

• Serves 8 •

4 eggs, separated

100 g/4 oz caster sugar

2 dessertspoons coffee powder

2 tablespoons boiling water

50 g/2 oz plain chocolate

1 tablespoon melted butter

4 tablespoons rum

150 ml/¼ pint double cream

chopped chocolate, chocolate beans or chopped nuts to decorate

Line a mould with cling film or similar. Whisk the egg yolks and sugar together until light and fluffy. Dissolve the coffee powder in the boiling water and leave to cool.

Melt the chocolate in a bowl over hot water and stir in the coffee, butter and rum. Stir this mixture into the yolks and sugar mixture. Whisk the cream until thick, and whisk the egg whites until stiff.

First fold the cream, then the whites into the mixture. Pour into the prepared mould and freeze for at least 4 hours. Turn out just before serving and carefully peel off the plastic film. Decorate with the chocolate, beans or nuts (or a mixture of them). (Do not turn out more than 10 minutes before serving.)

SHIRLEY WILLIAMS

Rich Chocolate Mousse

• Serves 4–6 •

6 eggs, separated

175 g/6 oz chocolate (half plain, half milk chocolate)

finely grated rind of 1 orange

1 dessertspoon orange juice

Beat the egg whites until they form stiff peaks. Break up the chocolate and melt very slowly (do this by putting the chocolate into a bowl and putting the bowl into a pan of simmering water). Beat the egg yolks with the orange rind and juice. When the chocolate has melted allow it to cool slightly and then mix it into the egg yolks. The mixture should be smooth and glossy. If it goes slightly lumpy, add a little milk and beat vigorously – this restores the texture. Then fold in the egg whites very gently using a metal spoon. Chill before serving.

Chocolate Peppermint Flan

• Serves 4 •

2 eggs

300 ml/½ pint milk

15 g/½ oz powdered gelatine

1 teaspoon cocoa powder

100 g/4 oz chocolate chips

150 ml/¼ pint double cream

2 drops peppermint essence

100 g/4 oz caster sugar

1 prepared biscuit case

Separate the eggs. Place the yolks, milk, gelatine, cocoa powder and chocolate chips in a bowl over hot water. Whisk until the mixture thickens slightly then remove and cool, stirring occasionally until just at setting point.

Whisk the cream with the peppermint essence. Whisk the egg whites until stiff but not dry, whisk in half the sugar, then fold in remainder. Gently fold into the chocolate mixture. Place alternative spoonfuls of each mixture into the flan case and swirl to give a marbled appearance. Leave until set. Serve cold.

• **Contributed by Sue Harrop** •
TTTE RAF Cottesmore

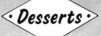
Pear and Almond Cream Flan

• Serves 6 •

1 egg and 1 egg white

50 g/2 oz caster sugar

40 g/1½ oz cornflour

1 teaspoon almond essence

450 ml/¾ pint milk

225 g/8 oz granulated sugar

900 ml/1½ pints water

3 pears, peeled and cored

juice of 1 lemon

a few toasted slivered almonds

Pastry

75 g/3 oz self-raising flour

25 g/1 oz cornflour

75 g/3 oz margarine

1 tablespoon caster sugar

½ teaspoon finely grated lemon rind

1 egg yolk

1–2 teaspoons water

Glaze

2 tablespoons apricot jam

1 tablespoon sugar syrup (from poached pears)

Make the pastry by sifting the flour and cornflour then rub in the margarine until the mixture resembles fine breadcrumbs. Stir in the sugar, lemon rind, egg yolk and enough water to bind. Line a 20-cm/8-in loose-bottomed flan tin and bake blind for 30 minutes in a moderate oven (180 C, 350 F, gas 4).

Beat the egg and egg white, sugar, cornflour and almond essence together. Heat the milk until warm. Pour over the mixture in the basin. Return the mixture to the pan, bring gently to the boil, stirring constantly. When the mixture thickens, simmer for 2 minutes. Cool slightly, then spoon into the cooked pastry case. Dissolve the granulated sugar in the water, add the lemon juice and poach the pears for 10 minutes. Drain on a wire rack. Arrange the pears in the flan case, pressing down in the custard cream. Sprinkle with the almonds. Melt the jam and syrup and use to glaze the flan. Chill.

Contributed by
• Lord and Lady Hertford •

Cherry Almond Flan

• Serves 4 •

175 g/6 oz shortcrust pastry

1 (390-g/13¾-oz) can cherry pie filling

Topping

50 g/2 oz butter

50 g/2 oz sugar

1 egg

3 drops almond essence

75 g/3 oz ground almonds

25 g/1 oz plain flour

Cream butter and sugar and add the egg and almond essence. Stir in the almonds and flour. Roll out the pastry and use to line a 20-cm/8-in pie dish. Fill with the pie filling and add the topping. Cook in a moderate oven (180 C, 350 F, gas 4) for 35 minutes.

Contributed by Mrs Audrey Mount •

Lemon and Raspberry Flan

• Serves 6 •

sweet shortcrust pastry

4 eggs

175 g/6 oz caster sugar

75 g/3 oz unsalted butter, softened

grated rind of 1 lemon

150 ml/¼ pint double cream

juice of 2 lemons

225 g/8 oz raspberries

Sauce

juice from raspberries

orange juice

Roll the pastry to 3 mm/⅛ in thickness and line a buttered 23-cm/9-in deep flan ring then chill. Beat together vigorously the eggs and sugar until the mixture turns a pale lemon colour. Beat in the butter and lemon rind. Fold in the cream and beat in the lemon juice. Fold in the raspberries.

Pour the mixture into the flan tin and place in a moderate oven (180 C, 350 F, gas 4) and bake for 40 minutes. Stand for 10 minutes before serving. Pour over a sauce made from the raspberry juice combined with orange juice.

• Contributed by Mr P J Shelton •

*L*ORD *K*ING OF *W*ARTNABY

❝ **I hope this will help with your endeavours for Leukaemia Research and I wish you success with the sale of the book.** ❞

Butterscotch Tart

• Serves 4 •

100 g/4 oz butter
....
100 g/4 oz demerara sugar
....
50 g/2 oz caster sugar
....
150 ml/¼ pint cream
....
1 cooked puff pastry flan case

Boil together the butter, both sugars, and cream until it drops from the spoon. Pour the mixture into the baked flan case and put into an oven for a few minutes to finish cooking. Serve with thick cream.

• **Obtained by Mr PJ Shelton** •

Pumpkin Pie

• Serves 4 •

100 g/4 oz brown sugar
....
100 g/4 oz white sugar
....
½ teaspoon salt
....
1 teaspoon ground ginger
....
1 teaspoon ground cinnamon
....
1 teaspoon ground cloves
....
350 g/12 oz canned pumpkin, drained
....
2 eggs, well beaten
....
1 cup milk or single cream
....
1 (23-cm/9-in) unbaked pastry case

Mix the dry ingredients together, then add the pumpkin, eggs and milk or cream. Pour into the pastry case. Bake in a hot oven (220 C, 425 F, gas 7) for 15 minutes, then reduce the temperature to moderate (180 C, 350 F, gas 4) and bake for 30 minutes longer.

• **Contributed by Stanley J Brown** •

Apricots in Port Wine

dried apricots

inexpensive port wine

Fill a jar with chopped apricots, pressing down well. Fill to the brim with port and cover tightly. Top up with more port from time to time. Keep at least six months. Serve with ice cream or Christmas pudding.

• Contributed by Mrs Angelia Pick •
Chairman of the School Governors

Lemon Cheesecake

• Serves 4–6 •

2 medium lemons

1 (170-g/6-oz) can evaporated milk

50 g/2 oz caster sugar

225 g/8 oz cottage cheese, sieved

175 g/6 oz plain chocolate, grated

mandarin and/or lemon slices

Crust

digestive biscuits

50 g/2 oz butter, melted

First make the crust by crushing the biscuits and adding the melted butter. Use this mixture to line the bottom of a pie dish or tin. Cool in fridge.

Meanwhile make the filling. Grate and squeeze the lemons. Whip the evaporated milk until very thick. Add the sugar, juice and rind of the lemons and the cottage cheese. Pour the filling on to the crust. Cool to set. Decorate with grated chocolate, mandarin and/or lemon slices.

• Contributed by Mrs Fox •

Baked Lemon Cheesecake

• **Serves 6–8** •

Mixture will be sufficient for one (28 cm × 18-cm/11 in × 7-in) Swiss roll tin or two (18-cm/7-in) sandwich tins.

shortcrust pastry
....
jam
....
Filling
....
100 g/4 oz margarine
....
100 g/4 oz caster sugar
....
2 standard eggs
....
100 g/4 oz ground rice
....
grated rind and juice of 1 lemon
....
100 g/4 oz currants
....
½ teaspoon freshly grated nutmeg

Line the Swiss roll or the two sandwich tins with shortcrust pastry. Spread with a thin layer of jam. Cream the margarine and sugar together, beat in the eggs and a little ground rice. Add the lemon juice then the rest of the ground rice and all the remaining ingredients. Spread this mixture into the tin or tins, pressing into the sides to seal. Cook in a moderately hot oven (190 C, 375 F, gas 5) for 35 minutes.

• **Contributed by Jean Harris** •

American Cheesecake

• **Serves 4–6** •

50 g/2 oz margarine, melted
....
1 small packet digestive biscuits
....
1 lemon jelly
....
225 g/8 oz caster sugar
....
300 ml/½ pint cream or cottage cheese
....
2–3 lemons
....
1 large tin evaporated milk

Make a biscuit base by mixing the melted margarine and crushed digestive biscuits. Chill well. Dissolve the lemon jelly in one cup of boiling water. Cool. Cream the sugar and cheese, add the juice of the lemons, and some grated rind. Chill the tin of evaporated milk, beat in an electric mixer until thick, fold in the cooled jelly, and pour over the biscuit base and chill well.

• **Contributed by Mrs Bevan** •

Special Trifle

• Serves 4 •

1½ packets trifle sponges
....
seedless jam
....
sherry to taste
....
75 g/3 oz flaked almonds
....
50 g/2 oz glacé cherries, chopped
....
600 ml/1 pint thick custard
....
150 ml/¼ pint double cream, whipped
....
ratafia biscuits
....
glacé cherries, angelica and blanched
almonds to decorate

Spread the trifle sponges, cut in half, with seedless jam. Sandwich together and arrange a layer in the bottom of a large bowl. Pour over 1 glass of sweet sherry. Sprinkle with half the nuts and cherries, chopped into pieces. Spread a layer of custard and repeat with a layer of sponge, etc. Add the rest of the custard and allow to set. Decorate the top of the trifle with the cream; put ratafia biscuits round the edge and decorate with glacé cherries, angelica strips and blanched almonds.

• Obtained by Mr P J Shelton •

Ginger Snow Queen

• Serves 4 •

450 ml/¾ pint double cream
....
2 tablespoons caster sugar
....
brandy to taste
....
175 g/6 oz broken meringue
....
4 pieces preserved stem ginger,
chopped
....
whipped cream to decorate

Whisk the cream until stiff then stir in the sugar, brandy and meringue. Pour into a lightly oiled pudding basin and freeze. To serve, first unmould the dessert, thaw in the fridge for about 30 minutes. Decorate with whipped cream.

Alternatives
Cointreau and oranges.
Brandy and raspberries or strawberries.

• Contributed by Elizabeth Chandler •
TTTE RAF Cottesmore

$\mathcal{A}$NNEKA $\mathcal{R}$ICE

Custard Ice Cream

• Serves 4 •

300 ml / 7 fl oz milk
....
1 tablespoon custard powder
....
2 tablespoons sugar
....
1 teaspoon vanilla essence
....
150 ml / ¼ pint double cream
....
1 egg white
....
wafers and fresh raspberries (optional)

Heat most of the milk to almost boiling. Mix the custard powder with the remaining milk, then stir in the hot milk. Bring to the boil slowly, stirring continuously. Simmer for 1 minute. Remove from the heat and beat in the sugar and vanilla essence. Cover and leave to cool. Whip the cream until thick, fold into the custard and pour into an ice tray. Freeze until fairly firm.

Take out of the freezer, and turn into a bowl and beat until smooth. Beat the egg whites until stiff and fold into the mixture. Return to the ice tray and freeze until hard. Serve with wafers and raspberries, if available.

• **Obtained by Joanne** •

❛ **The recipe book sounds a great way of raising money – I hope the book goes well.** ❜

Contributed by

the Mayoress of Charnwood

Jamaican Crunch Pie

• Serves 4 •

100 g/4 oz gingernuts, crushed

50 g/2 oz butter, melted

150 ml/¼ pint double cream

1 (198-g/7-oz) can sweetened
condensed milk

6 tablespoons lemon juice

grated rind of 1 lemon

Mix the crushed gingernuts with the melted butter and, with the back of a spoon, form a base in a 20-cm/8-in pie dish or plate. Put the remaining ingredients into a food processor, blender or bowl and mix well. Pour over the gingernut base and refrigerate overnight.

The Rt Hon

David Steel

MP

Athelbrose

• Serves 2–3 •

50 g/2 oz oatmeal

300 ml/½ pint double cream

2 tablespoons honey

whisky to taste

fresh fruit (optional)

Toast the oatmeal under a hot grill. Whip the double cream until thick. Add the oatmeal, honey and whisky to the cream and fold in. Fresh fruit, such as raspberries or loganberries, can also be added.

**‘ With best wishes
for a successful venture. ’**

Contributed by

. . . .

Nick Ross, Breakfast Time TV

. . . .

Zabaglione

• **Serves 1** •
Multiply the ingredients by
the number you wish to serve.

1½ egg yolks
. . . .
1½ tablespoons caster sugar
. . . .
1½ tablespoons Marsala
. . . .
little grated lemon peel (optional)

❛ **With all good
wishes for the enterprise.** ❜

Warm some glasses for serving. Put all the ingredients together in a large bowl (the mixture will expand). Use a double boiler or place the bowl over a saucepan containing boiling water.

Whisk the ingredients together, then take the bowl off the heat, and whisk, making sure to move the whisk around the edges of the bowl to stop the mixture setting unevenly. After a minute or two the contents will begin to expand into a light and frothy texture. Ladle into the warm glasses and serve immediately.

• **Obtained by Mr PJ Shelton** •

• BAKING •

Lemon Fridge Cake

• Serves 4 •

50 g/2 oz butter

75 g/3 oz caster sugar

2 eggs, separated

grated rind and juice of ½ lemon

1 packet sponge cakes

300 ml/½ pint whipping cream to decorate

Cream the butter and sugar together until white and soft then beat in the egg yolks, grated rind and juice of lemon. Whisk the egg whites until stiff and fold into the mixture.

Slice the sponges into quarters and line a 450-g/1-lb loaf tin. Fill with alternate layers of sponge and lemon mixture, finishing with a sponge layer. Cover and leave in the fridge for 12 to 24 hours. Turn out carefully on to a serving dish. Cover and decorate with piped-on whipped cream.

• **Contributed by Joyce Mackenzie** •

The Rt Hon

*M*ARGARET

*T*HATCHER

PM

Orange and Walnut Cake

• **Serves 6** •

225 g/8 oz self-raising flour

½ teaspoon salt

175 g/6 oz butter

175 g/6 oz caster sugar

3 large eggs, beaten

grated rind of 1 orange

25 g/1 oz chopped mixed peel

50 g/2 oz walnuts

1 tablespoon concentrated orange juice

Icing

225 g/8 oz icing sugar

2–3 tablespoons concentrated orange juice

Sift the flour and salt together. Cream the butter and sugar, and add the beaten eggs. Add half the flour and the other ingredients and blend. Add the rest of the flour. Spoon the mixture into an 18-cm/7-in greased cake tin and cook in a moderate oven (180 C, 350 F, gas 4) for 1¼ hours.

Warm the icing sugar and concentrated orange juice together in a pan until smooth. Ice the cake with this mixture while the icing is still warm. Be careful not to overheat the icing when blending.

• **Obtained by Ruth Gamble** •

American Carrot Cake

• Serves 4–6 •

225 g/8 oz plain flour

1½ teaspoons baking soda

1½ teaspoons baking powder

1 teaspoon ground cinnamon

150 g/5 oz sugar

100 g/4 oz walnuts or hazelnuts, finely chopped

1½ tablespoons sunflower oil

6 eggs

1 (227-g/8-oz) can crushed pineapple

225 g/8 oz carrots, grated

Frosting

225 g/8 oz Philadelphia cream cheese

100 g/4 oz butter

sifted icing sugar to taste

a few drops of vanilla essence

a little lemon juice (optional)

Mix the dry ingredients together then add wet. Pour into a greased tin. Bake for 35 to 40 minutes in a moderate oven (180 C, 350 F, gas 4) or till golden.

For the frosting, mix the ingredients till creamy, adding icing sugar to taste. Add a little lemon juice if too sweet. Use the frosting to decorate the top of the cake.

• Contributed by Gill Richardson •

Apple Sauce Cake

• Serves 6 •

350 g/12 oz cooking apples

1 tablespoon water

225 g/8 oz self-raising flour

pinch of salt

½ teaspoon baking powder

1 teaspoon ground mixed spice

175 g/6 oz margarine

175 g/6 oz caster sugar

2 eggs

50 g/2 oz walnuts, finely chopped

Grease an 18-cm/7-in round cake tin. Line the base of the tin with greaseproof paper. Grease the paper. Peel, core and slice the apples. Put in a small saucepan with the water. Stew for 5 minutes, until soft. Sieve the apples and cool. Sift the flour, salt, baking powder and mixed spice into a basin. Cream the margarine and sugar in a basin until light and fluffy. Add the eggs, one at a time, beating each in well. Fold the flour into the mixture, using a metal spoon. Stir in the apple sauce and the walnuts. Turn into the prepared tin and bake in the centre of a moderate oven (180 C, 350 F, gas 4) for 1¼ hours or until firm to touch and golden brown. Leave to cool in the tin for 10 minutes. Turn out on to a wire rack to cool. Sprinkle caster sugar on top of cake to decorate.

• Contributed by Theresa Hopkins •

Belgian Fudge Cake

• **Serves 4–6** •

100 g/4 oz butter
....
2 tablespoons golden syrup
....
225 g/8oz digestive biscuits, crushed
....
25 g/1 oz raisins
....
50 g/2 oz glacé cherries, quartered
....
150 g/5 oz Bournville chocolate, chopped

Fudge Icing

50 g/2 oz Bournville chocolate
....
25 g/1 oz butter
....
3 tablespoons water
....
175 g/6 oz icing sugar, sifted

To Finish

sifted icing sugar
....
melted chocolate
....
chopped cherries
....
whipped cream

First grease and base-line a 450-g/1-lb loaf tin. Melt the butter and syrup in a saucepan. Stir in the biscuits, fruit and chopped chocolate. Press firmly into the prepared tin and leave in a cool place to set. When it has set, turn it out on to a serving plate.

For the icing, melt the chocolate and butter with the water, over a gentle heat. Remove from the heat, stir in the sifted icing sugar and beat until cool and thick.

Spread the icing over the cake. Dust with icing sugar and decorate with extra melted chocolate and chopped cherries, if liked, and pipe whipped cream around the base.

Contributed by
• **Alistair and Elizabeth Dunn** •

Pineapple Cake

• **Serves 4–6** •

This cake is very
moist and keeps well.

350 g/12 oz mixed dried fruit
....
100 g/4 oz cherries
....
175 g/6 oz soft dark brown sugar
....
100 g/4 oz butter or margarine
....
1 (376-g/13¼-oz) can crushed
pineapple and juice
....
225 g/8 oz self-raising flour
....
2 eggs

Place the first five ingredients in a saucepan. Boil for 5 to 10 minutes. Stir occasionally. Leave to cool. Add flour and eggs. Mix together thoroughly. Bake for 1¾ hours in a moderate oven (180 C, 350 F, gas 4).

• **Contributed by Mrs Rosanna Ayres** •

Dundee Cake

• Serves 8 •

425 g/15 oz plain flour

1 teaspoon salt

75 g/3 oz glacé cherries

350 g/13 oz butter or margarine

350 g/13 oz caster sugar

7 large eggs

finely grated rind of 1 lemon

175 g/6 oz currants

175 g/6 oz sultanas

175 g/6 oz stoned raisins

75 g/3 oz chopped mixed peel

75 g/3 oz split blanched almonds

Grease and line a 23-cm/9-in cake tin with a double thickness of greased greaseproof paper. Sift the flour and salt into a mixing bowl. Wash and dry the cherries, then cut into quarters. Cream the butter or margarine with the sugar until light and fluffy. Beat in each egg with a tablespoon of sifted flour. Carefully fold in the remaining sifted flour and finely grated lemon rind, then gently stir in the dried fruits, cherries and peel until thoroughly mixed. Turn into the prepared tin, smooth over the top with a palette knife and arrange split almonds over the surface. Place the cake in oven on shelf below centre. Bake in a cool oven (150 C, 300 F, gas 2) for 2¾ to 3¼ hours. Allow to cool in the oven. Turn out and remove the paper.

• Contributed by Mr PJ Shelton •

'Never-Known-to-Fail' Fruit Cake

• Serves 6 •

350 g/12 oz mixed dried fruit

100 g/4 oz brown sugar

100 g/4 oz margarine

150 ml/¼ pint water

1 egg, beaten

225 g/8 oz self-raising flour

Place fruit, sugar, margarine and water in a saucepan and simmer slowly for 20 minutes. Allow to cool. Stir in the beaten egg then stir in the sifted flour. Tip into a greaseproof-lined 19-cm/7½-in cake tin and level the top. Bake in a cool oven (150 C, 300 F, gas 2) for 1¾ hours.

• Contributed by Susan Gamble •

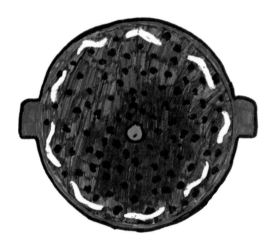

ROLF HARRIS

Banana Cake

• Serves 4 •

200 g/7 oz self-raising flour
....
2 teaspoons baking powder
....
¼ teaspoon baking soda
....
½ teaspoon salt
....
75 g/3 oz margarine or butter
....
150 g/5 oz sugar
....
2 eggs
....
2–4 over-ripe bananas

Sift together the dry ingredients. Cream the margarine, add the sugar and beat till pale and creamy. Add the eggs and beat in well. Add everything else and beat till all is well mixed up. (You can also add sultanas, dates, nuts or whatever.) Put the mixture into a greased tin and bake until done, about 1 hour or more, in a moderate oven (180 C, 350 F, gas 4), I think.

• **Obtained by Edward Shakespeare** •

Date Shortbread Cake

• Serves 6 •

225 g/8 oz butter

225 g/8 oz sugar

1 egg, beaten

350 g/12 oz plain flour

1 teaspoon cream of tartar

½ teaspoon baking soda

2 teaspoons ground cinnamon

225 g/8 oz dates, stoned and chopped

50 g/2 oz blanched almonds

sifted caster sugar to dust

Cream the butter and sugar together then add the beaten egg and the sifted dry ingredients. Spread a layer of the mixture over the bottom of two sponge tins. Cover this layer with a layer of chopped dates (squeeze flat with fingers). Now spread another layer of mix to cover the top of each tin. Dot with blanched almonds. Bake in a moderate oven (180 C, 350 F, gas 4) for about 30 to 35 minutes. When cool, dust with sifted caster sugar.

• **Contributed by Mrs Bevan** •

Rich Chocolate Cake

• Serves 4–6 •

2 eggs

100 g/4 oz margarine

100 g/4 oz caster sugar

100 g/4 oz self-raising flour

25 g/1 oz cocoa powder

1 teaspoon baking powder

Cream together the eggs and margarine and sugar. Add the sifted flour, cocoa powder and baking powder. Pour the mixture into two cake tins. Cook for 30 minutes in a moderately hot oven (190 C, 375 F, gas 5). Add your own topping, although my favourite topping is Dairy Milk chocolate decorated with Jelly Tots and Smarties.

• **Contributed by Oliver Taylor** •

Sacher Torte

• Serves 8 •

This famous cake was created in Vienna. The original recipe is a closely guarded secret. This adaptation was given to me by an Austrian family.

225 g/8 oz butter, softened

300 g/10½ oz caster sugar

6 eggs, separated

100 g/4 oz cocoa powder (or 4 squares melted bitter chocolate)

½ teaspoon salt

1 teaspoon vanilla essence

140 g/4½ oz self-raising flour, sifted

225 g/8 oz apricot jam, sieved

grated chocolate to decorate

Chocolate Icing

4 squares bitter chocolate

4 tablespoons double cream

425 g/15 oz icing sugar

pinch of salt

1 teaspoon vanilla essence

Cream the butter and 175 g/6 oz caster sugar until light and fluffy. In another bowl beat the egg yolks until thick. Gradually add the remaining sugar and beat for 5 minutes. Add the cocoa powder (or melted chocolate) to the creamed butter. Now beat the egg yolk mixture into the butter and beat for 5 minutes. Whisk the egg whites with the salt and vanilla essence until they form soft peaks. Gradually add the egg whites and flour to the butter mixture, a third at a time, folding in gently. *Do not overmix.* Grease and flour an 18-cm/7-in deep cake tin. Pour in the batter and level off. Bake in a moderate oven (180 C, 350 F, gas 4) for about 35 minutes. Place the cake on a wire rack for about 15 minutes. Whilst still warm brush the entire surface with apricot jam. Leave to cool for 2 hours.

Place the chocolate and cream in a small bowl, over boiling water, until the chocolate has melted. Mix well. Put the icing sugar and salt in a large bowl. Gradually add the melted chocolate. Beat well, adding more sugar if the mix is too thin to spread. Add the vanilla essence. Completely cover the cake with the chocolate icing. Decorate the top of the cake with grated chocolate.

• Contributed by Helen Tilson •

Contributed by

Blue Peter, BBC

Chocolate Easter Egg Cake

• Serves 6 •

275 g/10 oz self-raising flour

225 g/8 oz caster sugar

1½ teaspoons baking powder

1 (200-g/7-oz) jar mayonnaise

4 tablespoons cocoa powder

250 ml/8 fl oz boiling water

1 teaspoon vanilla essence

Icing

2 teaspoons instant coffee

2 tablespoons cocoa powder

2 tablespoons hot water

75 g/3 oz soft margarine

225 g/8 oz icing sugar

Sift the flour into a bowl and add the sugar and baking powder. Beat the mayonnaise well into the flour, sugar and baking powder – again it's very important to beat the mayonnaise thoroughly into the ingredients. Put to one side while you make the chocolate mixture.

Dissolve the cocoa powder in the boiling water. Stir gently until it's smooth and there are no lumps. Add the chocolate mix to the flour mixture (making sure that the flour mixture is well blended – it should look like large breadcrumbs). Give the whole mixture a quick stir and then add the vanilla essence. Stir everything thoroughly until all the ingredients are blended, but this time *don't* beat the mixture, because that will spoil it. Just keep stirring it gently until all the lumps are gone. Line an 18-cm/7-in cake tin with greaseproof paper, greasing the tin side of the paper, otherwise it will stick to the tin. Put the tin into the middle of a moderate oven (180 C, 350 F, gas 4) and cook for about 1 hour. To make sure it's baked all through, test it with a knitting needle – if it comes out cleanly, then it's cooked. Leave the cake to cool in the tin before turning it out. The cake is now ready for icing.

Dissolve the coffee and cocoa powder in the hot water. Add the soft margarine and icing sugar. This time beat the mixture thoroughly, ensuring that no lumps are left, and then spread the mixture over the cake. This amount is enough to cover the top of the cake and all round the sides.

To make a professional job and for a finishing touch you can add little sugar eggs and if you have a tiny fluffy chicken you can put that on top of the cake.

Lincolnshire Plum Bread

• **Serves 4–6** •

100 g/4 oz butter

100 g/4 oz demerara sugar

2 eggs

¾ teaspoon ground cinnamon

½ teaspoon ground mixed spice

1 tablespoon brandy

½ teaspoon gravy browning

pinch of salt

200 g/7 oz self-raising flour

100 g/4 oz sultanas

100 g/4 oz currants

100 g/4 oz soaked prunes, finely chopped

Cream together the butter and sugar. Beat in the eggs, spice, brandy and gravy browning. Sift the salt and flour together, add to the mixture with the dried fruit and finely chopped prunes. Pour the mixture into a greased and lined 900-g/2-lb loaf tin. Bake in a cool (140 C, 275 F, gas 1) oven for 3 to 3½ hours. Turn out when cool.

• **Contributed by Theresa Hopkins** •

The Rt Hon

$\mathcal{N}$ORMAN $\mathcal{F}$OWLER

MP

Banana Bread

• Makes a 450 g/1 lb loaf •

100 g/4 oz butter

225 g/8 oz brown sugar

1 egg

2 ripe bananas

225 g/8 oz wholewheat flour

1½ teaspoons baking powder

1 teaspoon salt

4 tablespoons natural yogurt

Beat the butter and sugar together thoroughly, then beat in the egg. Mash the bananas and mix them in. Sift together the flour and baking powder then add the salt. Mix half the yogurt into the banana mixture, then half the flour. Then the rest of the yogurt and flour. Mix in well. Grease a 450-g/1-lb loaf tin well and put the mixture in. Bake in a moderate oven (180 C, 350 F, gas 4) for 1 hour.

• Obtained by Mr P J Shelton •

❝ May I wish you success in your fund raising for a very worthwhile cause. ❞

Almond Tartlets

• Makes 18 •

225 g/8 oz shortcrust pastry

about 5 tablespoons jam

100 g/4 oz caster sugar

100 g/4 oz ground almonds

50 g/2 oz semolina

100 g/4 oz icing sugar

1 egg and 1 egg white

a few drops of almond essence

Roll out the pastry and cut into 18 round tart shapes. Place in greased patty tins and put a little jam in each. Mix the dry ingredients together. Stir in the remaining ingredients and use to cover the tarts. Bake in a hot oven (220 C, 425 F, gas 7) for 20 minutes.

• Contributed by Gail Compton •
TTTE RAF Cottesmore

Jump for Joys

• **Makes about 10** •

25 g / 1 oz margarine

2 tablespoons sugar

6 teaspoons golden syrup

2 tablespoons cocoa powder

50–75 g / 2–3 oz cornflakes

Place the margarine, sugar, syrup and cocoa powder into a saucepan, stir and bring to the boil for 1 minute, then gradually stir in the cornflakes and mix well. Put into paper cases until set.

• **Contributed by Lady Boardman** •

Ginger Iced Oatcake

• **Makes about 16** •

100 g / 4 oz margarine

2 tablespoons golden syrup

225 g / 8 oz rolled oats

2 teaspoons ground ginger

100 g / 4 oz soft brown sugar

Icing

1 teaspoon ground ginger

6 tablespoons icing sugar

75 g / 3 oz margarine

3 teaspoons water

Brush a Swiss roll tin with melted margarine or butter. Melt the margarine and syrup in a saucepan and add the dry ingredients. Pack into the tin and level the surface. Bake for 15 to 20 minutes in a moderate oven (180 C, 350 F, gas 4).

Melt all the ingredients for the icing in a pan and pour over the oatcake. Leave to cool and cut into squares.

• **Contributed by Mrs Audrey Mount** •

Caramel Shortcake

• **Makes 20–24 pieces** •

100 g / 4 oz butter

50 g / 2 oz caster sugar

175 g / 6 oz self-raising flour

plain or milk melted chocolate to cover

Caramel

100 g / 4 oz margarine

100 g / 4 oz sugar

2 tablespoons syrup

1 (170-g/6-oz) can sweetened condensed milk

First make the base, cream the butter and sugar together then add the flour, mix well. Roll out lightly and press into a well greased Swiss roll tin. Bake in a moderate oven (160 C, 325 F, gas 4) for about 30 minutes.

To make the caramel, boil all ingredients together for 4 minutes only, pour over the shortcake and leave to cool. Cover the shortcake with melted chocolate.

• **Contributed by Georgina Hodges** •
TTTE RAF Cottesmore

Coconut Ice

• Makes 24 squares •

8 tablespoons condensed milk

350 g/12 oz icing sugar

175 g/6 oz desiccated coconut

a few drops of cochineal food colouring

1 tablespoon cocoa powder

Mix the milk and icing sugar together then stir in the coconut. Divide the mixture in half. Add colouring to one amount. Spread this in an 18-cm/7-in square cake tin. Sift the cocoa into the remaining mixture and stir well. Spread on top of the pink and set overnight. Cut into squares.

• Contributed by Mrs Audrey Mount •

Chocolate Crispies

• Makes about 20 •

3 Mars bars

75 g/3 oz butter

75 g/3 oz Rice Crispies

about 50 g/2 oz plain or milk chocolate

Melt the Mars bars and butter over a gentle heat. Stir in the Rice Crispies. Press into a tin lined with non-stick baking parchment. Melt the chocolate in a bowl over hot water. Spread over the crispie mixture, make a design with a fork and leave to set.

• Contributed by Lynne Harris •
TTTE RAF Cottesmore

Chocolate Fudge Bars

• Makes 450 g/1 lb •

100 g/4 oz margarine

2 tablespoons syrup

175 g/6 oz caster sugar

1 small tin Nestlé's milk

200 g/7 oz digestive biscuits, crushed

200 g/7 oz melted chocolate to cover

Melt the margarine, syrup, sugar and Nestlé's milk together and simmer for 8 minutes, stirring frequently. Remove from the heat and beat for 2 minutes. Add the crushed biscuits and stir well. Put into a greased Swiss roll tin and cover with the melted chocolate, when cool.

• Contributed by Sarah Rimmer •
TTTE RAF Cottesmore

Afghan Biscuits

• **Makes about 50 biscuits** •

675 g/1½ lb margarine
....
450 g/1 lb caster sugar
....
575 g/1¼ lb plain flour
....
40 g/1½ oz baking powder
....
50 g/2 oz cocoa powder
....
225 g/8 oz cornflakes
....
chocolate drops to decorate

Cream the margarine, sugar and cocoa powder together and add the remaining ingredients. Roll the mixture into balls. Place on a greased baking tray, flatten slightly and leave room for spreading. Cook in a moderate oven (180 C, 350 F, gas 4) for about 20 minutes, or until lightly browned. Place a chocolate drop on top as they come out of the oven.

• **Contributed by Mrs Doig** •

HRH THE PRINCESS OF WALES

Fudge

• **Makes about 50 squares** •

450 g/1 lb sugar
....
50 g/2 oz butter
....
4 tablespoons water
....
1 (397-g/14-oz) can sweetened condensed milk

Put the sugar, butter and water into a large saucepan (preferably a non-stick saucepan). Stir gently until the sugar is dissolved. Add the condensed milk and bring to the boil. Simmer on a very low heat until the mixture thickens and browns – this should take about 30 minutes. Stir occasionally during simmering. Remove from the heat and beat well. Pour into a greased tray. Wait until it is set and then cut into squares.

Oatmeal Biscuits

• Makes about 25 biscuits •

2 teaspoons golden syrup

1 tablespoon milk

75 g/3 oz margarine

75 g/3 oz self-raising flour

75 g/3 oz caster sugar

75 g/3 oz oats

½ teaspoon bicarbonate of soda

Put the golden syrup, milk and margarine into a saucepan and heat until the margarine has melted. Add the other ingredients and mix well. Put teaspoons of this mixture on a well greased baking tray. Bake in a moderately hot oven (190 C, 375 F, gas 5) for 5 minutes.

Contributed by

Blue Peter, BBC

Mrs Maligrandi's Biscuits

• Makes between 48–60 biscuits •

150 g/5 oz margarine

1 large egg

225 g/8 oz self-raising flour

150 g/5 oz caster sugar

100 g/4 oz desiccated coconut

glacé cherries to decorate (optional)

Put the margarine and egg into a large mixing bowl and stir together. Add the flour, sugar and desiccated coconut. Give all the ingredients a quick stir and then blend them together with your hands until the mixture forms a soft and fairly sticky dough. Roll out on a floured board to 5 mm/¼ in thick, then cut out biscuit shapes and place on a greased baking tray. Bake in the centre of a moderate oven (160 C, 325 F, gas 3) for 20 minutes. Add glacé cherry to the top, if desired.

Chocolate Peppermint Biscuits

• Makes about 12–16 biscuits •

100 g/4 oz margarine

1 tablespoon sugar

1 tablespoon golden syrup

2 tablespoons cocoa powder

225 g/8 oz digestive biscuits, crushed

Topping

75 g/3 oz butter

150 g/5 oz icing sugar

a few drops of peppermint essence

a few drops of green food colouring

75 g/3 oz plain chocolate, melted

Slowly melt the margarine, sugar and syrup. Remove from the heat and stir in the cocoa powder. Mix together well with the biscuits and press firmly into a shallow greased tin. Leave to set. Meanwhile, make the topping. Cream the butter and icing sugar together. Add peppermint essence and green colouring to taste. Spread the topping evenly over the cooled biscuit mixture and top with the melted chocolate. Cut into squares when set.

• Contributed by Mrs E Kirby •

Dame
Janet Baker

❛ **These are the best ginger biscuits in the world!** ❜

Ginger Biscuits

• Makes between 60–70 biscuits •

225 g/8 oz margarine

450 g/1 lb self-raising flour

225 g/8 oz brown sugar

2 teaspoons ground ginger

225 g/8 oz golden syrup

Rub the margarine into the flour. Add the sugar, ground ginger and warmed syrup. Place on a greased baking tray and leave to set overnight. Bake in a moderate oven (180 C, 350 F, gas 4) until brown.

Wagga Waggas

• Makes about 20 biscuits •

175 g/6 oz butter or margarine

75 g/3 oz icing sugar

175 g/6 oz plain flour

25 g/1 oz custard powder

Cream the butter and sugar together. Stir in the flour and custard powder and work to a smooth dough. Roll into balls the size of a walnut. Space well apart on a greased baking tray and flatten slightly with a fork. Bake for 20 minutes in a moderate oven (160 C, 325 F, gas 3).

• Contributed by Mrs Bevan •

PAUL DANIELS

Brandy Snaps

• Makes 35 •

100 g/4 oz butter

100 g/4 oz golden syrup

100 g/4 oz sugar

100 g/4 oz flour, sifted

½ teaspoon ground ginger

1 tablespoon brandy

whipped cream to fill

Melt the butter, syrup and sugar in a saucepan. Add the flour, ginger and brandy. Put a teaspoonful of the mixture on to greased baking trays (at least 7.5 cm/3 in apart). Bake for 10 minutes in a moderate oven (160 C, 325 F, gas 3). Remove from the tray with a knife and roll round the handle of a wooden spoon while still warm. When cold the brandy snaps are delicious if filled with whipped cream.

• Obtained by Simon Burgess •

Chocolate Fruit Bars

• Makes 12–16 squares •

75 g/3 oz butter

1 tablespoon golden syrup

225 g/8 oz muesli or Alpen

25 g/1 oz raisins, chopped

50 g/2 oz glacé cherries, chopped

100 g/4 oz plain chocolate, melted

Melt together the butter and syrup. Add the muesli, raisins and cherries. Stir in well. Press the mixture into an 18-cm/7-in square tin lined with greased greaseproof paper. Allow to cool, then pour on the melted chocolate. When cold, cut up into squares.

• Contributed by Mrs G Belton •

· GEOFFREY SMITH ·

Home-made Bread

• Makes 4 (450-g/1-lb) loaves •

| 675 g/1½ lb wholewheat flour |
| 675 g/1½ lb unbleached white flour |
| 1 teaspoon salt |
| 25 g/1 oz dried yeast |
| 1 teaspoon sugar |
| 3 tablespoons warm water |
| 2 tablespoons oil |
| 1 large tablespoon molasses |

Mix together the flours and salt in a large mixing bowl and put to warm. Mix the yeast with the sugar in a little warm water in a jug and leave to prove (froth) for about 10 minutes. When the yeast starts to froth, make a hollow in the flour and pour in the yeast mixture, together with the oil and the molasses which should be dissolved in tepid water. It should take about 600–900 ml/1–1½ pints of liquid. Stir the mixture at first then, as it stiffens, work it with the hands and knead the dough for a few minutes till all is worked in. Place the mixture in a warm place to rise.

When the mixture has risen to about twice the original size, cut it into four pieces and knead each piece for a minute or two to form loaves. Place in well-greased bread tins and put to rise again. When the dough has risen to the top of the tins, bake in a moderately hot oven (200 C, 400 F, gas 6) for 30 to 45 minutes.

❛ This recipe for home-made, wholemeal bread is, as we say in Yorkshire, "Very More-ish" indeed. I think a recipe book is a splendid idea – may I be your first customer? ❜

· CONTRIBUTORS ·

Alexander, Jean (Hilda Ogden)
Andrews, Eamonn
Ayles, Peter J
Ayres, Rosanna

Bacon, Jim
Baker, Dame Janet
Ball, Bobby
Barker, Ronnie
Bates, Simon
Bellamy, David
Belton, Mrs Gwendoline
Bennett, Lennie
Bevan, Mrs
Blue Peter, BBC
Boardman, Lady
Boehnke, Angelika
Boy George
Brown, Stanley
Buccleuch and Queensberry, Duke of

Cannon, Tommy
Canterbury, Archbishop of
Chandler, Elizabeth
Charnwood, Mayoress of
Chiavolini, Enrica
Coe, Sebastian
Compton, Gail
Corry, Peggy
Cotton, Bill
Craven, John
Creedy, Jan

Daniels, Paul
Davis, Steve
Dawson, Les
Doig, Mrs
Dougherty, Maggie
Dunn, Alistair and Elizabeth

English, Arthur

Foster, Averil
Fowler, The Rt Hon Norman, MP
Fox, Mrs Jennie
Francini, Viviana
Francis, Clare

Gamble, Susan
Gloucester, Duchess of
Goodson, Alan
Green, Betty
Gretton, Lord and Lady

Harris, Jean
Harris, Lynne
Harris, Rolf
Harrop, Sue
Haywood, Colonel T C S
Herriot, James
Hertford, Lord and Lady
Hird, Thora
Hodges, Georgina
Hogg, Mrs L
Hopkins, Theresa
Hoppe, Vera
Humperdinck, Engelbert

Inman, John

Joint, Julia

King, Lord, of Warnaby
Kinnock, The Rt Hon Neil, MP
Kirby, Mrs E
Knox-Johnson, Robin

Latham, The Rt Hon Michael, MP
Lawley, Sue
Lawson, The Rt Hon Nigel, MP
Leeming, Jan
Leicester, Bishop of
Linneker, Gary

Lockwood, Fiona
Long, Janice

McCartney, Paul
Mackenzie, Joyce
Major, Anne
Mansell, Nigel
Middleton, Pat
Milne, Gordon
Missarina, Anna
Montagu, Lord, of Beaulieu
Moorcroft, David
Mount, Mrs Audrey
Mount, Mrs Joyce

Officers' Mess, RAF Cottesmore
Officers' Mess, RAF North Luffenham
Owen, The Rt Hon Dr David, MP

Pasch, Waltraut
Peacock-Pochin, Elizabeth
Pick, Angelia
Pollard, Su

Rantzen, Esther
Read, Mike
Reagan, Mrs Nancy
Reagan, President Ronald
Renzo, Ama Di
Rice, Anneka
Richard, Cliff
Richardson, Gill
Rimmer, Sarah

Ross, Nick
Rutland, Duchess of

Sheene, Barry
Shelton, Mr P J
Sibson, Tony
Smith, Geoffrey
Staff, Kathy
Steel, The Rt Hon David, MP
Storer, June
Swain, Elizabeth

Tavistock, Marquess of
Taylor, Oliver
Thatcher, The Rt Hon Margaret, PM
Thompson, Daley
Thorpe, Judy
Tilson, Helen
Tonypandy, Viscount
Torville and Dean
Tubi, Maria Grazia

Wadsworth, Tony
Wales, HRH Princess of
Wales, HRH Prince of
Wallington, Mark
Wellington, Duchess of
Wells, Olive
Wells, Sister Pauline
Wheeler, Peter
Williams, The Rt Hon Shirley, MP
Wogan, Terry
Wood, Dr J K

INDEX